FOUND

Biblical Wisdom For The Questions We All Ask

metamorphosis
PUBLISHERS

OBED OLIVARRÍA

Cover design by Obed Olivarría

Typeset and inside design by Obed Olivarría

Library of Congress Control Number: 2024925855

ISBN (print edition): 978-1-966179-88-7

ISBN (eBook edition): 978-1-966179-00-9

First Edition: August 2025

Metamorphosis Publishers.

Santa Ana, California.

For information contact:

http://www.obedolivarria.com

Contents

Introduction: The Eternal Quest for Answers

O NE EVENING, AS THE last bit of sunlight slipped below the horizon, I found myself alone with my thoughts under a canopy of stars. I was walking around the park in our neighborhood, and everything was still, except for the occasional hum of a distant car or the chirp of bugs. There's something grounding about staring into the night sky, where countless pinpricks of light stretch into infinity. In that moment, I felt an almost ancient ache—a familiar tug that seems to show up during life's quietest moments. I wasn't thinking about my to-do list or the routine stress of everyday life. Instead, my mind had turned to something deeper, a question that had followed me through different seasons: "What's the purpose of it all?" And then other questions followed.

I wondered if, maybe, I wasn't alone in these questions. The world, after all, is filled with people just like me, people who seek meaning, connection, and answers. Countless philosophers, writers, and poets throughout human history have spent lifetimes wrestling with questions about life, purpose, and existence. We ponder our significance in the universe, the reason behind suffering, the nature of love, and the purpose of faith. These aren't the kinds of questions we bring up in everyday conversation. They're quieter, like a soft whisper that lingers in the background, surfacing when we're still.

That night, as I gazed up at the stars, I realized that these questions weren't just an accident of our human curiosity. They're invitations—questions woven into the very fabric of who we are, guiding us to seek something greater. And, like many others before me, I had begun to suspect that the answers were waiting in a place I hadn't fully explored yet. You see, over the years, I've seen people respond to these questions in different ways. Some try to silence them with distractions—work, social media, or endless to-do lists. I sure did! Others dive into self-help books, hoping to find themselves through productivity and personal growth. But in that moment, I began to suspect that the answers I was looking for wouldn't be found on my own. They would be found in the words of a God Who's been whispering (and sometimes shouting) answers to His people for thousands of years.

Scripture is more than a collection of ancient stories. It's a wellspring of wisdom, filled with people just like us who wrestled with the same questions, who grappled with doubt, sought purpose, endured suffering, and, through it all, encountered a God Who spoke into their lives. So, thinking there under the stars, I made a decision: I was going to seek those answers, not in the things I could accomplish or the people I could impress, but in the words of a God Who has always known us, loved us, and seen us as His own.

Why We Question

Why do we ask questions? It's not just curiosity; it's often driven by a deeper need—a search for meaning. Questions are birthed from our longing for connection, understanding, and assurance. They arise when we encounter moments of doubt or wonder, when life doesn't make sense, or when we feel overwhelmed by the challenges we face. Often, these questions are spurred by pain, loss, or a sense of emptiness. Other times, they arise from moments of great joy or success when we wonder what's next in our journey.

Questions are an inherent part of being human. From the moment we first gain the ability to form words, we begin asking them. "Why is the sky blue?" "Where does the sun go at night?" As children, we bombard the world with our curiosity, hungry for knowledge, eager for answers. As we grow older, the questions may change, but the yearning for understanding does not. Instead, the questions deepen: "Why do bad things happen to good people?" "Where is God in my suffering?" "How do I find peace in the chaos of life?" These are no longer questions that can be answered with a quick explanation—they are questions of the soul.

Biblical Wisdom

And why use the Bible as a guide? Well, simply put, because there is power in biblical wisdom. The Bible isn't just a historical record—it is a living document that speaks to the human condition in every generation. Through its stories, teachings, and examples, it provides a framework for understanding not only the world, but also ourselves. The wisdom found in Scripture offers insight into our purpose, our identity, and the very nature of existence.

But what exactly is wisdom? Unlike knowledge, which is simply the accumulation of facts, wisdom is the application of that knowledge in a meaningful way. It is the ability to make sound decisions, to navigate life's complexities with grace and understanding, and to live in alignment with God's truth. Biblical wisdom takes this a step further by grounding us in eternal truths that transcend culture, circumstance, and time. It offers us principles by which we can live, providing clarity when life feels uncertain.

Throughout the Bible, we see countless examples of people grappling with questions and seeking wisdom. From Job's heartfelt cries in the midst of suffering to David's psalms of praise and lament, to Solomon's quest for understanding, the Bible shows us that asking questions is not only natural but necessary. And it shows us that in every season of life, God is ready and willing to offer us His wisdom—if only we will ask.

There is a stark comparison between the outcomes of wise and foolish decisions. King Solomon alludes to this, and Jesus adds to it using the parable of the wise and foolish builders. Wise decisions, grounded in the fear of God and obedience to His commands, lead to blessings, stability, and favor. At the same time, there are pitfalls and long-term consequences of decisions made in folly, without regard for God's principles.

Wisdom is not just an intellectual pursuit, but a matter of the heart that affects our desires, motivations, and ultimately our decisions. Wisdom is both a gift from God and a pursuit that requires action on our part—found through prayer, reflection, and immersion in Scripture. Wisdom is not just for the 'big' decisions in life, but it is also essential for navigating the complexities and challenges of everyday life. Biblical wisdom can be applied in various scenarios, offering readers relatable situations and actionable advice. In fact, there are benefits in making decisions based on wisdom, including peace of mind, improved relationships, and alignment with God's purposes.

I encourage you to continuously seek wisdom in all areas of your life. It is a lifelong journey that enriches our walk with God and leads to a more fulfilling and impactful life. Foster a mindset of learning and growth rather than guilt. Pursue wisdom diligently as the path to a fruitful and God-honoring life. Use Scripture as your tool in everyday decisions and immerse yourself in Scripture as the primary source of wisdom and guidance.

Commit to a lifelong journey of seeking Biblical wisdom, by cultivating a wise heart and regularly self-examination in light of Scripture, commitment to godly community, and persistent prayer for God to grant His wisdom generously.

What This Book is About

In Found: Biblical Wisdom for the Questions We All Ask, we will embark on a journey to explore some of life's most profound and challenging questions. These are the questions that linger in the back of our minds when we are faced with uncertainty, fear, and suffering. They are the questions that surface in times of joy and in moments of despair. At their core, these questions are not just about understanding the world around us—they are about understanding ourselves, our purpose, and our relationship with God.

Found is an invitation to journey with me through the Bible as we explore answers to some of life's deepest, most universal questions. This book is for those who want to dig deeper, who want to find hope and peace not in the fleeting solutions the world offers, but in the enduring wisdom of Scripture.

The Bible is the source of wisdom that has guided countless generations through these very questions. It is not just a book of ancient stories or a collection of religious rules. It is a divine compass, a treasure trove of wisdom, providing answers to the deepest longings of our hearts. Scripture addresses not only the "what" and the "how" but also the "why." It speaks to our need for purpose, our search for identity, our longing for peace, and our desire for justice. And, most importantly, it reveals a God who is not distant or detached but intimately involved in our lives—loving, guiding, and providing answers when we seek Him.

So, in this book, using Scripture as a guide, we'll tackle questions like "Who am I?" and "Why am I here?" We'll explore themes of identity, purpose, suffering, peace, and perseverance—questions that don't just float around in our minds, but often define how we live. We will look at what the Bible has to say about the challenges we face, the suffering we endure, and the hope we long for. We will see that the Bible does not shy away from hard questions, nor does it offer easy, surface-level answers. Instead, it invites us into a deeper relationship with God, where we can wrestle with these questions and ultimately find the wisdom, peace, and direction we seek.

In the pages that follow, we will walk through some of life's most pressing questions. Each chapter is an invitation to wrestle with these questions honestly, trusting that God has already woven answers into His Word. This journey is divided into three parts, and each part of this book builds on the next, forming a path that can guide us toward a life of peace, purpose, and faith.

Part 1: The Foundation of Our Existence

Here, we'll start by looking at core questions of identity, purpose, and worth. This foundational part offers answers that anchor us as we navigate the challenges of life. We'll explore the big questions: Who are we? Why are we here? What is the purpose of our existence? These are the questions that shape the way we view ourselves and the world around us.

Part 2: Navigating Life's Challenges

Life is filled with trials and challenges, from personal suffering to global injustices. In this section, we'll confront some of life's tough realities, like suffering, pain, and finding peace. We'll ask tough questions like: Why do we suffer? Where is God in our pain? How do we find peace in troubling times? These are the questions that confront us when life seems overwhelming, and they demand deep, thoughtful answers. These chapters are designed to help us approach life's storms with a renewed perspective and a source of hope.

Part 3: The Journey of Faith

Faith is not static; it's a journey filled with ups and downs, moments of doubt, and times of great assurance. In this final section, we'll explore questions like: How do we trust God in uncertainty? How should we live in light of our faith? What role does community play in our spiritual growth? These are the questions that guide us in living out our faith each day. The final part explores what it means to live out our faith with perseverance, trust, and the strength of community. This is where we learn to live out what we believe, with practical wisdom and encouragement for every step of the journey.

How to Use This Book

The journey we're embarking on together is not about having all the answers right away. It's about seeking, exploring, and discovering. It's about being honest with ourselves and with God about our struggles, our doubts, and our fears. It's about recognizing that wisdom is not something we achieve but something we receive—a gift from God that comes when we ask in faith.

So, as we begin this journey, I invite you to open your heart, your mind, and your spirit to what God has in store. Let's approach these questions not as problems to be solved but as opportunities for growth. Let's trust that the One Who created us is also the One Who can guide us through the complexities of life. And in that seeking, may we find what we've been searching for all along: the wisdom that comes from above, the peace that surpasses understanding, and the assurance that we are never alone on this journey.

This isn't just a book to read; it's a book to experience. At the end of each section within each chapter, you'll find reflection questions and exercises. These aren't homework assignments; they're opportunities designed to help you dig deeper into the topic at hand. I encourage you to pause, think, and even pray through these exercises. In other words, take time with these questions, wrestle with them, and invite God into your process of reflection. After all, the journey to wisdom is not a sprint; it's a marathon, one that requires patience, perseverance, and a willingness to embrace the unknown. Consider keeping a journal where you can record your reflections, your questions, and your discoveries.

Let's go on this journey together. Let's wrestle with the hard questions and discover the answers that God has laid out for us. My prayer for you as you read is that you won't just find answers; you'll find hope, peace, and a renewed sense of purpose. Because the truth is, the answers we're searching for aren't as far off as they seem. They're already here, waiting for us to discover them.

Welcome to Found—may you discover the wisdom you need and the answers you seek.

PART 1

THE FOUNDATION OF
OUR EXISTENCE

Chapter 1

Who Am I? Understanding Our Identity

Created in God's Image

WHEN I WAS A kid, I was absolutely convinced that I was destined for greatness. You could say I had an unwavering belief in my own potential—and honestly, it was kind of endearing. I was the kid who thought he could grow up to be an astronaut or the president, and I had no reason to believe otherwise. As I continued growing, I was convinced that I'd do something big one day. Not necessarily something famous, but something *meaningful*. Maybe I'd travel the world, help people in need, or discover something amazing. I was confident in myself, and in my own unique way, I believed I had something special to offer the world.

Fast forward a few decades, and life has a way of shaking that confidence. Suddenly, I found myself measuring my worth against how I stacked up to others. Instead of feeling unique, I often felt ordinary. I'd see people doing things I thought were out of reach, and I started wondering if my value was tied to what I could accomplish. I think we've all been there: wondering if we're good enough, smart enough, *special* enough. By the time I hit my twenties, I had gone from feeling like a unique individual to feeling like just another face in the crowd. The world had a way of reminding me that I wasn't the smartest, the best-looking, or the most successful, and somewhere along the way, I began to doubt that I had any unique value at all.

Then, one night, after a particularly rough week during college, I opened my Bible and found myself reading Genesis 1:27: "*So God created mankind in His own image, in the image of God He created them; male and female He created them.*" I stopped. Even though it was a very familiar verse, I read it again. And it hit me as if I'd never read it or heard it before. I realized that I am created in the image of God. That means my worth doesn't come from my job, my achievements, or my appearance. My worth is something far deeper—it's embedded in my very being, given to me by the One Who created me. And I realized that understanding my identity in Christ is crucial for a confident and purposeful life.

This idea of being made in the image of God, or *imago Dei*, is one of the most foundational truths of our existence and it is central to understanding who we are. According to Genesis, every single one of us is created with a unique imprint of God's own nature. We're not defined by our titles, our bank accounts, or our talents. We're defined by something much more profound: we reflect the image of God Himself. Our identity rooted in the very nature of God, and that is where our value comes from. We are God's masterpiece, created anew in Jesus to do the good works God prepared in advance for us. Realizing this is our identity is what brings value and purpose to our lives.

This truth means that every person, regardless of race, status, age, or ability, has inherent worth and dignity. Our identity isn't something we earn; it's something we already possess. And this changes everything. When we understand our identity as God's image-bearers, we can live with a sense of purpose and confidence, knowing that our worth is secure in Him. Society may try to tell us that our worth is in our looks, our achievements, or our social status, but God tells us something different. He tells us that our worth is inherent. We're His creation, bearing His image, and that alone gives us intrinsic value. Knowing this can change how we see ourselves and others, allowing us to see beyond the labels the world tries to impose on us. We must see ourselves as God sees us. And our true worth is found not in the world's eyes, but through our reflection in the 'mirror' of God's Word.

The Bible is filled with verses that speak to the value God places on His creation. Psalm 8:4-5 captures this beautifully: "*What is mankind that you are mindful of them, human beings that you care for them? You have made them a little lower than the angels and crowned them with glory and honor.*" This doesn't mean that we're perfect; we're far from it. But it does mean that our identity is rooted in something unshakeable.

The story of Adam and Eve in Genesis is a powerful example of this truth. When God created them, He didn't give them value based on their abilities or achievements. He gave them value simply because they were His. And that same truth applies to us today. No matter how much we struggle or how far we feel we've fallen, we still carry that sacred imprint of God's image.

Reflection Questions

- *How does knowing you're created in God's image shape your understanding of your worth?*

- *Have you ever placed your identity in things other than God? How has that affected your life?*

Reflection Exercise

Take a few minutes to journal about a time when you felt closest to your true self. What was it about that moment that made you feel whole? Reflect on how that experience aligns with the idea of being made in God's image. Consider writing a short prayer, asking God to help you see yourself as He sees you.

Identity Distorted by Sin

God calls us into a journey of unveiling and living out this masterpiece identity, including recognizing our uniqueness, embracing God's call, and impacting the world around us. Unfortunately, our spiritual identity can be 'stolen' or obscured by life's challenges, societal labels, and personal failures. Losing sight of our identity in Christ impacts our spiritual health and life direction. It's hard to admit, but many of us chase every source of validation we can find. We want people to think we are successful, talented, and well-liked.

We carefully curate social media posts, present ourselves in ways we think people will admire, and at times, we even work ourselves to the bone just to keep up appearances. We are constantly performing, like chameleons, adjusting how we act depending on who we are with, always looking for approval. We change our colors to fit whatever we think will win the most praise. It's exhausting!

But listen, no matter how much effort we put into crafting this image and no matter how much we perform, we will never feel satisfied. We won't shake the emptiness this way. In fact, the more we seek validation from others, the emptier we will feel. It's like trying to fill a bottomless pit, one that can never be filled by likes, promotions, or praise. In chasing these things, we only lose sight of who we really are, trying to fit into a mold that the world has created instead of the one God intended for us.

The Bible teaches us that this sense of disconnection is part of the human condition. Sin distorts our sense of self, leading us to find our identity in things that were never meant to define us. Romans 3:23 reminds us, *"For all have sinned and fall short of the glory of God."* This verse is a humbling reminder that, because of sin, we often place our worth in things that cannot truly satisfy us.

When we search for identity in things outside of God, we become like people staring into distorted mirrors, unable to see our true reflection. Society constantly encourages us to seek our value in external things: wealth, status, beauty, and achievements. But these things are fleeting, and when they inevitably fade or disappoint us, we're left questioning who we are.

The story of the fall in Genesis 3 shows us how sin distorts our relationship with ourselves, each other, and God. When Adam and Eve chose to disobey God, they introduced a kind of brokenness that affected not only their relationship with Him but also their understanding of themselves. They became ashamed, covering themselves and hiding from God. This is the effect of sin—it creates a disconnection, a sense of inadequacy and shame that pulls us away from our true identity as God's image-bearers.

Reflection Questions

- *In what ways have you sought your identity in things outside of God, and how has that impacted you?*

- *What steps can you take to begin seeing yourself as God sees you, rather than through the lens of worldly achievements?*

Reflection Exercise

Spend a few moments in prayer, asking God to reveal any areas of your life where you've been looking for worth in places other than Him. Write down what comes to mind and reflect on how you can begin to shift your focus back to your identity in Christ.

Restoring Identity in Christ

I remember sitting in a church pew one day, feeling completely bored out of my mind. I had been a Christian all my life, but I was going through a season where I just didn't feel close to God. I'd been struggling with doubts and a nagging feeling that I wasn't "enough." Then, as the pastor began his sermon, he read from 2 Corinthians 5:17: *"Therefore, if anyone is in Christ, the new creation has come: The old has gone, the new is here!"*

Those words hit me like a wave. *New creation.* It was a reminder that, in Christ, my identity wasn't something I had to build or achieve. It was something that had already been given to me. I didn't need to earn God's love or prove my worth; it was already secure. That moment sparked a journey of rediscovering who I was in Christ, and it brought a kind of peace I hadn't felt in a long time.

The beauty of the Gospel is that Christ doesn't just forgive us; He gives us a new identity. In other words, the gospel is not just forgiveness; it is transformation. Through faith, we become "new creations" with a fresh start and a restored purpose. Galatians 2:20 captures this transformation perfectly: *"I have been crucified with Christ and I no longer live, but Christ lives in me."*

This means that in Jesus we are no longer defined by our past mistakes, failures, or shortcomings. Our identity is secure in a Savior, Who loves us and calls us His own. In Him, we find a confidence that is unshakable, a purpose that is eternal, and a worth that doesn't depend on anything we can achieve. And we have a call to reflect Christ's image in our lives; this is a central aspect of our identity in Him. This mandate must be applied and reflected in all aspects of our lives—personal behavior, relationships, and work.

One of the most powerful examples of transformation in the Bible is the story of Saul, who became Paul. Saul was a man who persecuted Christians, yet after encountering Christ on the road to Damascus, his life was radically transformed. He went on to become one of the greatest apostles, spreading the Gospel and living out his new identity in Christ. Paul's story reminds us that no matter how far we feel we've wandered, God can and does redefine who we are. So, live a life of boldness and purpose, armed with the knowledge of your identity in Christ.

Reflection Questions

- *What does it mean to you to be a "new creation" in Christ?*

- *How can you live more confidently in your identity as a beloved child of God?*

Reflection Exercise

Write a prayer asking God to help you embrace your identity as His child. Ask for strength to let go of past hurts and false identities, and to live boldly in the knowledge that you are a new creation in Him.

Chapter 2

Why Am I Here? Discovering Our Purpose

Created with Purpose

WE OFTEN FIND OURSELVES asking, "Why am I here?" This is the foundational question of human existence. The Bible teaches that we are not random accidents, but rather intentional creations of a loving God. Our existence is rooted in His divine purpose. The biblical understanding of Creation demonstrates that every person was designed with meaning and purpose. From the beginning, God planned for us to have a relationship with Him, to reflect His image, and to fulfill a specific role in His grand design

Genesis 1:26-27 says, "*Then God said, 'Let us make humankind in our image, in Our likeness, so that they may rule over the fish in the sea and the birds in the sky, over the livestock and all the wild animals, and over all the creatures that move along the ground.' So, God created humankind in His own image, in the image of God He created them; male and female He created them.*"

The creation of Adam and Eve (Genesis 1:26-31, Genesis 2:7-9, 18-25) is the first great narrative of purpose. God formed Adam from the dust of the Earth and breathed life into him, setting him in the garden of Eden to work it and take care of it. He was given dominion over all creation, tasked with naming the animals, and given Eve as a companion to help fulfill his purpose. From the very beginning, we see that humanity was created with intentionality and responsibility.

That is why the psalmist said in Psalm 139: 13-14, *"For You created my inmost being; You knit me together in my mother's womb. I praise You because I am fearfully and wonderfully made; Your works are wonderful, I know that full well."* And then Jeremiah added in Jeremiah 29:11, *'For I know the plans I have for you,' declares the Lord, 'plans to prosper you and not to harm you, plans to give you hope and a future.'"*

From these verses, we can learn a few things. First, we learn that we are made in God's image. This means that our worth is intrinsic, and our purpose is divine. We reflect God's character, love, creativity, and stewardship. We also learn that we are created for relationship. Just as Adam and Eve were made for each other and for communion with God, we are designed for meaningful relationships—with God and with others.

Also, God has a specific plan for each of us. God's plan is not generic; it's tailored to each individual's gifts, talents, and calling. Our purpose is multifold. One of these things is to steward the Earth. Humanity was placed in charge of creation to manage it responsibly, showing that part of our purpose involves caring for the world and the people around us. And lastly, our identity comes from God. Our identity is rooted in being God's creation, not in external achievements or circumstances.

Created in God's Image

By understanding the major movements in Scripture—Creation, Fall, Redemption, and Restoration—we see how our personal stories intersect with the divine story. The Bible is full of characters who discovered their purpose within God's narrative. From Moses leading the Israelites out of Egypt to Paul spreading the gospel across the ancient world, these stories illustrate how an individual's life can significantly impact the broader story of God's people. Let's start at the beginning.

In the grand narrative of Creation, one of the most profound statements made is that humanity is created in God's image. This notion isn't just a theological gem tucked away in Scripture; it's a vibrant truth that shapes our identity and purpose. Imagine for a moment: the Creator of the universe, the One Who spun galaxies into existence, decided to stamp a piece of His essence on us.

Being created in God's image means we have inherent value and dignity. Every time we look in the mirror, we should see a reflection of the divine spark that resides within us. It's not about the perfect hair or the latest fashion—though a good outfit can certainly boost confidence! Instead, it's about recognizing that we carry the fingerprints of our Creator.

But this is not just a warm and fuzzy feeling; it's a call to action. When we acknowledge our worth, we can't help but treat others with the same respect and love. After all, if we're all made in His image, the person next to you—yes, even that guy who just cut you off in traffic—holds the same divine potential.

God, the ultimate Artist, didn't just create a cookie-cutter mold for humanity. Instead, He crafted each of us with unique talents, passions, and quirks—like a divine bouquet of flowers, each with its own color and fragrance! Embracing our individuality means celebrating our differences rather than letting them divide us. God's image is multi-faceted and wonderfully diverse. So, when you find yourself comparing your gifts to someone else's, remember that you are a crucial part of the masterpiece. Your unique contribution is essential to the bigger picture.

Being made in God's image comes with responsibilities. Being image-bearers means we are called to reflect God's character in our daily lives. This means kindness, love, and justice are not just optional; they're foundational to our identity. Every act of compassion, every moment of forgiveness, and every effort to seek justice are like brushstrokes on the canvas of our lives, painting a picture of Who God is to the world around us. When we embody these qualities, we become living testimonies of His grace and goodness.

As we navigate life's challenges, understanding that we are created in God's image equips us for the journey. It reassures us that we are never alone; we have the Creator walking alongside us, guiding us with wisdom and love. When doubts creep in and the world tries to diminish our worth, we can stand firm on this truth: we are fearfully and wonderfully made. So, let's embrace our divine identity with joy and confidence, knowing that we are not just surviving, but thriving as reflections of our magnificent Creator. With every step we take, let's shine brightly and show the world the beauty of being made in God's image.

Fallen, but Not Forgotten

If we are created with purpose and in God's image, then why do we experience brokenness and pain? The Bible answers this question through the narrative of the fall of humanity. Sin disrupted our relationship with God, ourselves, others, and creation. Yet, despite this fall, God did not abandon us. His purpose for us remains intact, and His plan to restore us was set into motion even before the foundations of the world.

Romans 3:23 says that *"for all have sinned and fall short of the glory of God."* The story of Adam and Eve's fall in the Garden of Eden (Genesis 3:1-24) reveals the tragic moment when sin entered the world. Deceived by the serpent, they chose to disobey God, breaking the perfect harmony they had enjoyed with Him. This act of rebellion had far-reaching consequences: death, toil, pain, and a severed connection with their Creator. Yet, even in this moment of devastation, God offered a promise of hope—the coming of a Savior Who would one day defeat evil and restore what had been lost.

Unfortunately, sin distorts our identity. In the grand tapestry of life, our identities are often stitched together by the threads of our experiences, beliefs, and choices. Yet, when sin enters the picture, it can feel like a mischievous monster has taken to pulling those threads, resulting in a design that is anything but beautiful. This distortion can lead us to view ourselves through a warped lens, obscuring the divine image in which we were created.

The struggle with identity distortion isn't a new phenomenon; it's as ancient as humanity itself. Think back to Adam and Eve, who, after their little escapade in the garden, suddenly felt the weight of shame and fear. Instead of embracing their God-given identity, they hid among the trees, convinced they were unworthy. Sound familiar? Sin often convinces us to hide—whether it's behind busyness, bitterness, or even perfectionism. We forget that God delights in us, not because of our perfection, but because we are His.

It's crucial to recognize that while sin can distort our view of ourselves, it doesn't change God's perspective. He sees us as beloved, cherished, and worthy of grace. In Ephesians 2:10, we're reminded that we are God's handiwork, created for good works. This means our identity is not defined by our missteps, but by His purpose for us. Embracing this truth can be like turning on a light in a darkened room; suddenly, the shadows of self-doubt and guilt fade away, revealing the bright and beautiful identity that has always been ours.

Sin also distorts our purpose. Sin broke the original design God had for us, introducing suffering, pain, and separation from Him. The consequence of the fall are universal. That means that every human experiences the effects of sin, both personally and collectively. This brokenness is why the world is filled with injustice, suffering, and conflict. But thankfully, God's plan for redemption began immediately. Even as He delivered judgment after the fall, God promised a solution—the Messiah—Who would crush the serpent and bring restoration.

This is important because our identity can only be restored through Christ. Though sin marred our identity, Jesus' sacrifice offers a way to be reconciled to God and rediscover our true purpose. And because of this, the fall does not define us any longer. While we live in a fallen world, our destiny is not determined by it. God's purpose for us remains, and through Christ, we are invited back into relationship with Him.

Redeemed for a Greater Purpose

While sin may have disrupted God's original design, His plan for redemption reaffirms our purpose. Through Jesus, we are not only restored to right relationship with God, but we are also given new meaning and mission. 2 Corinthians 5:17 says, "*Therefore, if anyone is in Christ, the new creation has come: The old has gone, the new is here!*" So Christ restores our identity and out purpose.

Restoring Identity in Christ is like finding that missing puzzle piece that suddenly brings clarity to the whole picture of your life. Imagine rummaging through a box of old toys, only to find that long-lost action figure you adored as a kid. That rush of nostalgia and joy is akin to rediscovering who you are in Christ. Too often, we let the world, our past mistakes, or even our daily struggles dictate our sense of self. But the gospel offers a radical reset button, inviting us to embrace our true identity as beloved children of God.

Restoring your identity in Christ also means letting go of the labels that the world sticks on you. Whether it's "failure," "overachiever," or "nobody," these labels can weigh us down like a backpack full of bricks. But God has a knack for redefining us! He sees beyond our flaws and failures, calling us "forgiven," "loved," and "redeemed." The journey of restoring our identity in Christ is not a one-time event, but a beautiful, ongoing process. Think of it as a delightful dance, where we learn the steps with grace and joy, occasionally stumbling but always getting back up.

The story of Paul's conversion on the road to Damascus (Acts 9:1-19) is a powerful example of how God redeems and repurposes a life. Paul, once a fierce persecutor of Christians, was dramatically transformed by an encounter with Jesus. His newfound faith led him to become one of the greatest apostles, spreading the gospel to the Gentiles. This transformation shows that no matter our past, God can use us for His glory and greater purpose.

Redemption through Jesus restores our identity. Through Him, we become new creations, redeemed from the brokenness of sin and restored to our rightful place as children of God. And now, we are called to a mission. Every believer is called to be an ambassador of Christ, sharing the message of hope and reconciliation with the world. Though we are not saved by good works, good works are a natural response to the grace we have received. So, our lives are to glorify God, since our ultimate purpose is to reflect God's glory in all we do, pointing others to His love and truth. Every experience can be redeemed. Even our past mistakes, pain, and brokenness can be used by God to fulfill His purpose in our lives.

The Great Commission and Our Purpose

I remember a time, years ago, when I felt utterly lost in life. After a major career change and having to go back to school for a post-graduate degree, I was temporarily working a job that, while paying the bills, didn't exactly fill me with passion. I'd wake up, head to work, come home, and repeat. One Friday night, I found myself sitting alone with glass of water, staring out the window at a world that felt like it was moving while I was standing still. I thought to myself, *Is this it? Is this all I'm here for? Because if that is it, then it sure sucks.*

I knew well that the job was temporary, and that the current situation was circumstantial. I forgot to add that this was also during pandemic, so this didn't help. But the feeling was real. It was a frustrating realization, one that left me questioning everything. I wanted my life to matter and to feel like I was making a difference in the world, but I had no clue where to start.

That weekend, I found myself flipping through the book of Matthew, where I landed on Matthew 28:19-20—the Great Commission: *"Therefore go and make disciples of all nations, baptizing them in the name of the Father and of the Son and of the Holy Spirit, and teaching them to obey everything I have commanded you."* Reading it, I felt a nudge in my spirit. This purpose wasn't about a career, title, or achievement; it was about something far greater. It was about living for a mission that extended beyond me.

Understanding our purpose begins with the recognition that, as followers of Christ, we are called to a greater mission. The Great Commission—Jesus' directive to go and make disciples of all nations—is a purpose that applies to every believer. This doesn't mean everyone is called to leave home and become a missionary in a foreign country. But it does mean that our lives are meant to reflect God's love, truth, and grace in the places where He has placed us.

The Bible shows us that purpose is more than a career or set of accomplishments. It's a calling to live in a way that points others to God. When we understand that our purpose is rooted in God's mission, our lives take on a new significance. It becomes less about the "what" and more about the "why." Each day becomes an opportunity to live out this calling, whether it's in our relationships, our work, or our interactions with strangers.

The concept of purpose in the Bible is both universal and personal. Jesus' Great Commission in Matthew 28:19-20 is a universal purpose given to all His followers, but Scripture also shows us that each person's life is uniquely designed to glorify God in specific ways. Take the story of Esther, for example. Esther was placed in a position of influence "*for such a time as this*" (Esther 4:14), and she fulfilled her purpose by using her position to save her people.

This story reminds us that God works through our circumstances and roles, even when they seem mundane or unimportant. Even when they're temporary! And whether we're in a high-profile position or serving quietly in the background, God has a purpose for each of us that ties into His greater plan.

As we reflect on the Great Commission and our purpose, let's embrace the joy of being part of something bigger than ourselves. This divine call isn't just about ticking off a checklist; it's about weaving our lives into the fabric of God's kingdom. With every conversation, every act of love, we get to be the hands and feet of Jesus, bringing His light into the dark corners of the world.

Reflection Questions

- *How does knowing that you were created with purpose change the way you view your life and your role in the world?*

- *What does the Great Commission mean to you personally? How can it shape your understanding of your purpose?*

- *Are there unique roles or circumstances in your life where you feel God might be calling you to live with greater purpose?*

Reflection Exercise

Take a moment to reflect on the areas of influence God has given you. It might be your family, workplace, church, or community. Write down how you can bring a sense of purpose to each of these areas, aligning your actions with the Great Commission. Ask God to open your eyes to opportunities to reflect His love and truth in these settings.

Living Purposefully Every Day

Living purposefully every day is like embarking on a grand adventure where each moment is an opportunity to discover the divine plan laid out for us. Imagine waking up each morning, not just to a routine, but to a treasure hunt where the prize is fulfilling God's purpose in your life. As Christians, we are called to embrace each day with enthusiasm, knowing that every moment can be infused with meaning and intention. With a sprinkle of joy and a dash of faith, we can transform the mundane into something extraordinary.

Living purposely starts with a heart open to God's guidance. Before you dive into your day, take a moment to pray and seek divine insight. Ask God to reveal opportunities where you can shine His light. Whether it's lending an ear to a friend in need, volunteering at a local charity, or simply sharing a smile with a stranger, these small acts can ripple out and create waves of purpose. Living purposefully doesn't always mean grand gestures; sometimes, it's the little things that matter most.

When I was in college, we met an older woman from one of the local churches, who would walk around the neighborhood saying hi to everyone. Everyone in the community knew her by name. This was a woman who seemed to carry purpose in everything she did. She didn't exactly accomplish anything the world would call "extraordinary," but she was well-known in the community for whom she was and what she did. Every time one interacted with her, one could feel a quiet strength, a sense of peace. She cooked meals with love, listened with compassion, and seemed to notice the details that most of us miss. She knew many of the neighbors by name and was the first to offer a helping hand. She never went on grand adventures or sought the spotlight, but she lived each day intentionally, with purpose and kindness.

When she passed away, people from all walks of life came to her funeral. They spoke of how she had impacted their lives in small but meaningful ways. This reminded me that purpose wasn't about grand gestures. It was about how she lived every day, with intention and love. It made me think: *What if purpose is less about what we achieve and more about how we live, day by day?*

Purpose isn't always about a singular, dramatic calling. Sometimes, it's about the small acts of faithfulness and love that we show in our everyday lives. The Bible teaches us that God values faithfulness in the little things, just as much as He values faithfulness in the big things. As 1 Corinthians 10:31 reminds us, *"So whether you eat or drink or whatever you do, do it all for the glory of God."*

This verse speaks to the idea that our purpose can be woven into the simplest aspects of life. Every action, no matter how routine, can be an opportunity to live with purpose when we do it with a heart that seeks to honor God. This can (and should be) done whether at work, school, or playing.

The story of Ruth is a powerful example of this truth. Ruth wasn't a queen or prophet; she was a widow who chose to remain faithful to her mother-in-law, Naomi, in a foreign land. Her daily acts of kindness, loyalty, and hard work became part of a much larger story—one that ultimately placed her in the lineage of Jesus. Ruth's life shows us that purpose can be found in the ordinary, in small, faithful acts that seem insignificant, but hold deep meaning in God's eyes.

Understanding your purpose is both a discovery and a decision—a decision to live in alignment with God's design. Intentional living and taking the small steps that lead to significant breakthroughs empowers us to embark on a life lived with purpose, aligned with God's grand design. And let me tell you, there is a transformative power in living a life aligned with God's purpose! Our deepest passions often point towards our divine purpose. And aligning our interests with God's will leads to a fulfilling and impactful life.

Embark on this journey of purposeful living. While the path may be challenging, the reward is a life of profound meaning and divine fulfillment. Envision the potential impact of your contributions to God's kingdom. Consider the legacy you wish to leave. And make intentional choices that reflect you purpose.

Reflection Questions

- *What are some ordinary tasks you do daily that could reflect God's purpose?*

- *How can you bring a sense of intentionality and faithfulness to your interactions and responsibilities?*

- *What are some specific ways you can live out your purpose as a redeemed child of God in your daily life?*

Reflection Exercise

Take a moment to list three areas of your life where you could live with greater purpose. These might be small, everyday activities, or they could be relationships that need more intentionality. Write down one simple action you can take for each area to reflect God's love and presence. For instance, "I will make an effort to speak words of encouragement to my coworkers" or "I will take five minutes each morning to pray for my family." Come up with some of your own.

Overcoming Obstacles to Purpose

There are common obstacles, such as fear, doubt, and the distractions of daily life, that can derail our pursuit of purpose. By acknowledging these challenges upfront, we set the stage for a deeper understanding and practical strategies for overcoming them. In fact, in the grand tapestry of life, we often encounter diverse obstacles that feel like unwelcome party crashers at our divine celebration of purpose. These challenges can come in various forms—uncertainty, dread, and even the occasional existential crisis. A few years ago, I was considering a major life decision. I felt God calling me to take a leap of faith, but the fear of failure held me back. My mind was flooded with doubts: *What if I fail? What if this doesn't work out? What if I'm just making things up in my head?* The more I thought about it, the more paralyzed I became. This decision would involve uprooting my family, moving, changing careers, getting more in debt, going back to school, and going into the unknown.

One night, as I wrestled with this decision, I came across Romans 8:28: *"And we know that in all things God works for the good of those who love Him, who have been called according to His purpose."* That verse reminded me that God's purposes don't rely on my ability to be perfect or having all the answers. They rely on His ability to work through my imperfections and doubts. It was a humbling moment, but also freeing. I realized that if I trusted God, I could take that step, not because I was confident in myself, but because I was confident in Him.

Accepting God's calling and living out our purpose isn't always easy. There are often obstacles—fear, doubt, and distractions—that make us question whether we're really capable of making a difference. But the Bible encourages us to trust that God is with us and that He will work through us, even when we feel inadequate.

Romans 8:28 reminds us that God is able to use every situation, even our failures, for His greater purpose. Jeremiah 29:11 further assures us, *"For I know the plans I have for you... plans to prosper you and not to harm you, plans to give you hope and a future."* These verses teach us that God's purposes aren't limited by our weaknesses; they're strengthened by His grace.

The story of Moses offers a powerful example of someone who struggled with doubts yet went on to fulfill a remarkable purpose. When God called Moses to lead the Israelites out of Egypt, Moses was reluctant. He doubted his own abilities, saying, "Who am I that I should go to Pharaoh and bring the Israelites out of Egypt?" (Exodus 3:11). But God's response was simple and profound: *"I will be with you."* Moses' story teaches us that God's presence and guidance are greater than any obstacle.

Living A Life of Legacy

I don't know about you, but I would love to be remembered for something positive when I am no longer here. And I believe most of us do as well. Think of legacy from a perspective of purpose. Consider how you wish to be remembered and the impact you desire to leave on the world. A legacy of purpose is not built on accomplishments alone, but on the lives touched, the love shared, and the light of God's love spread to others.

What are some practical ways to build a lasting positive legacy? I can think of several: investing in relationships, mentoring others, and contributing to causes that align with God's kingdom. Start taking steps toward your legacy today, no matter where you are in your journey of purpose. Realize the importance of each choice and action you take in crafting a legacy that honors God and inspires others to pursue your God-given purpose.

A great way to start is by identifying how you can be of service, with your specific God-given gifts and talents. Ask yourself: What unique gifts have I been blessed with? How can I use my time, gifts, resources, and talents to serve others?

The call to service is a biblical mandate, which illustrates how serving others not only enriches communities, but also provides personal fulfillment and spiritual growth. So, I encourage you to dive deep into self-reflection, understanding that identifying your God-given talents is the first step toward living with purpose and legacy. Uncover the passions and abilities that resonate with your soul, as these lay the groundwork for a life of intention and fulfillment.

Once you've done that, then identify opportunities for service that align with your talents and passions. Connect with community groups, nonprofits, and ministry programs that resonate with your skills and calling. Volunteerism, mentorship, and other forms of giving back, underscore the transformational impact of service on both the giver and the receiver. Explore the depths of your potential, which are often hidden beneath layers of routine, self-doubt, and societal expectations. Step out of your comfort zones to discover and unleash these dormant abilities. But take the first step, no matter how small, towards service.

And do all of this with gratitude, not for self-glorification. There are long-term benefits in service and altruism all while maintaining a positive and grateful outlook, including improved mental and spiritual health, deeper relationships, and a heightened sense of purpose.

Now, sometimes you must go through a process of trial, error, and exploration in various aspects of life, including career, hobbies, and spiritual practices in order to find your niche. So, adopt a mindset of curiosity and openness to new experiences. Remember that there is a transformative power when one embraces their true full potential.

Reflection Questions

- *What fears or doubts are holding you back from embracing your purpose?*

- *How can trusting in God's promises help you overcome these obstacles?*

Reflection Exercise

List three obstacles that you feel are preventing you from living out your purpose. Next to each obstacle, write a prayer, asking God for the strength, courage, or wisdom to overcome it. For example: "Lord, help me overcome my fear of failure by remembering that Your strength is made perfect in my weakness." Use these prayers as a reminder to trust in God's promises whenever these obstacles reappear.

Chapter 3

What is My Worth? Understanding Value from a Biblical Perspective

You Are Precious in God's Eyes

PICTURE THIS: GOD, WITH all His majesty, takes a moment to gaze upon you. He doesn't see your flaws or failures; instead, He sees your potential, your heart, and the incredible journey you are on. This perspective is crucial when life throws its curveballs. When you're feeling down, remember that even on your worst days, you are still beloved. God's love isn't contingent on your performance; it's a constant, like the North Star guiding you home. So, when you feel like a misplaced sock in the laundry of life, remind yourself that you're actually a rare collector's item in God's treasure chest.

I'll never forget a conversation I had with a friend during one of the toughest seasons of my life. I was going through a time of setbacks, and nothing I tried seemed to work out. After weeks of frustration and discouragement, I finally admitted to my friend that I felt like a failure, as if my worth was slipping away with each failed attempt. My friend looked at me and said, "You know, your worth doesn't come from what you do. It comes from who you are."

That simple statement stopped me in my tracks. Could it really be true? I had always thought of myself as someone who was valuable because of what I accomplished. But now, faced with my own limitations, I was forced to confront a deeper question: *What if my worth had nothing to do with my successes or failures?*

In that moment, I was reminded of Isaiah 43:4, where God says, *"Since you are precious and honored in My sight, and because I love you."* God's love for us isn't contingent on our achievements; it's rooted in His unwavering love and the value He places on each of us.

If you are precious in God's eyes, it means you have inherent value that doesn't fluctuate based on your circumstances. Think of it like a priceless painting. Even if it's covered in dust or gets a little tear, its worth remains unchanged. You are that masterpiece, crafted with intention and love. You are simply you, and that is more than enough! Embrace this truth and watch how it transforms the way you interact with the world around you.

Our worth isn't something we earn; it's something God has given us. Isaiah 43:4 emphasizes that we are precious and honored in God's sight, not because of anything we've done, but simply because He loves us. This understanding is both freeing and transformative. It means that our identity isn't defined by our job title, social status, or even our past mistakes, and our worth and value doesn't depend on our accomplishments, our status, or the approval of others. It is a gift from God, woven into the fabric of who we are as His children.

This divine perspective changes everything. If we can grasp that our worth is grounded in God's love, we can free ourselves from the endless cycle of striving for validation. Instead, we can live confidently, knowing that our identity is secure in Him.

Being precious in God's eyes is not just about how He sees you; it's about how you can see yourself. When you recognize your own worth, it empowers you to face life's challenges with confidence and grace. You stop comparing yourself to others, realizing that your journey is uniquely yours. You become a radiant light, shining brightly in a world that often feels dark and dreary. And, oh boy, does the world need your light.

The Bible contains numerous verses that affirm our worth in God's eyes. Matthew 10:29-31, for instance, says, *"Are not two sparrows sold for a penny? Yet not one of them will fall to the ground outside your Father's care... So don't be afraid; you are worth more than many sparrows."* This passage reminds us that God is intimately aware of each detail of our lives. If He cares for even the sparrows, how much more does He care for us?

The Parable of the Lost Sheep (Luke 15:1-7) offers another glimpse into our value in God's eyes. When one sheep goes missing, the shepherd leaves the ninety-nine others to find the lost one. This story illustrates that God values each of us individually and will go to great lengths to bring us back to Him. Our worth isn't based on our performance but on God's loving pursuit of us.

Reflection Questions

- *When have you felt most aware of your worth in God's eyes?*

- *How does understanding that God values you independently of your achievements change your view of yourself?*

Reflection Exercise

Take a moment to write down three qualities that you believe God values in you—not based on achievements, but on who you are as His child. Reflect on how these qualities reflect the love and worth God has given you. As you go through your week, use this list as a reminder of your inherent value in God's eyes.

Worth Beyond Worldly Standards

A while back, I found myself caught in a comparison trap. I was scrolling through social media, looking at all the "perfect" lives everyone seemed to have—exciting high-paying jobs, their own beautiful homes in areas my family can't afford, countless adventures, perfect-looking families. And there I was, wondering why my own life didn't measure up, even though I worked so hard. I started questioning my decisions, my goals, even my life decisions which had shaped my identity. Was I worth any less because I didn't have the same accomplishments or accolades?

Thankfully, before I sank deeper into this mindset, I remembered a comforting verse, 1 Samuel 16:7: "*The Lord does not look at the things people look at. People look at the outward appearance, but the Lord looks at the heart.*" This verse reminded me that God's measure of worth is different from the world's. My value wasn't based on how my life looked on the outside, but on the love and purpose God had given me on the inside.

In a world that often measures worth by wealth, status, or the latest gadget, it's refreshing to remember that true value isn't found on a price tag or a social media follower count. Consider the parable of the lost sheep from the Gospel of Luke. Here's a shepherd who leaves ninety-nine sheep to search for just one that's gone astray. Now, if we were to add up the numbers, it seems a bit impractical, doesn't it? But therein lies the beauty! Each sheep is valued equally, teaching us that our worth is intrinsic and not contingent on how others perceive us. In God's eyes, whether you're a high-flyer in the corporate world or the quiet hero volunteering in your community, you are worth the same—infinitely precious.

The world often places value on things that are temporary—appearance, success, wealth, and popularity. But these things can change in an instant. God, on the other hand, values what is lasting and true. He doesn't judge us by outward standards; He sees our hearts, our intentions, and our faithfulness.

Psalm 139:14 reminds us that we are *"fearfully and wonderfully made."* This isn't just a nice sentiment; it's a profound truth about our inherent worth. We are valuable not because of how we look or what we achieve, but because of the intentional care and creativity God poured into each of us. He sees past the external layers and knows the person He created us to be.

The story of Gideon in Judges 6 is a powerful example of how God values us beyond worldly standards. When God called Gideon to lead Israel against the Midianites, Gideon saw himself as insignificant, saying, *"My clan is the weakest in Manasseh, and I am the least in my family"* (Judges 6:15). But God saw something in Gideon that Gideon couldn't see in himself. He saw a "mighty warrior," someone He could use for His purposes.

Gideon's story teaches us that our worth isn't defined by our social status or background. God calls us according to His vision for us, not the world's view of us. And in the same way, God sees worth in each of us, even when we feel inadequate or overlooked.

As Christians, we're called to challenge societal norms, and that means flipping the script on what it means to be successful and valuable. The world tells us that our worth is tied to our accomplishments, but the Bible reveals a different narrative. The Apostle Paul, for instance, counted all his achievements as loss for the sake of Christ (Philippians 3:8). What a mind-bending perspective! By redefining success through a spiritual lens, we can find joy in the smallest acts of love and service, proving that true worth is often found in the least expected places.

So, as we navigate life's challenges, let's carry with us the playful reminder that our worth is not defined by the world. Instead, it's rooted in our identity as beloved children of God. We are valued for who we are and not what we have or what we've done. When we embrace this truth, we unlock a life of purpose, joy, and connection that transcends worldly measures. So go ahead, wear your worth like a crown, because in the eyes of the Divine, you are indeed a masterpiece!

Reflection Questions

- *How have you seen yourself through worldly standards, and how has that affected your self-worth?*

- *What might it look like to begin seeing yourself through God's perspective instead?*

Reflection Exercise

Identify an area in your life where you've been measuring your worth by worldly standards. Take a few minutes to write down why this area is important to you and how it affects your self-image. Then, read Psalm 139:14 and ask God to help you see yourself as *"fearfully and wonderfully made."* Reflect on what it means to release worldly standards and embrace God's view of your worth.

Living in Confidence of God's Value

When I was in college, I ran a ministry made up of college students, in which we would travel each weekend and do ministry at churches, camps, parks, or wherever we were invited. I remember one time one of my friends there said something to me that made me sad. She said that she felt deeply insecure about sharing her faith. She thought that if she wasn't perfect, then she had no right to talk about God or do any type of ministry. One evening, during a small group discussion, she shared this struggle. I remember God inspiring me at that moment, and I looked at her and said, "Your value isn't in how perfectly you represent God; it's in the fact that He loves you, flaws and all."

After the meeting she shared that these words felt like a weight lifting off her shoulders. She realized that her confidence didn't have to come from her own abilities. It could come from the unshakable truth of God's love and value for her. This newfound confidence allowed her to share her faith more openly, not because she felt worthy on her own, but because she was finally trusting in God's worth in her.

When we truly understand our worth in God, it changes the way we live. Knowing that we're valuable in God's eyes frees us from needing approval from others, allowing us to live boldly and confidently. Romans 8:37-39 reassures us that nothing can separate us from the love of God, and Ephesians 2:10 reminds us that *"we are God's handiwork, created in Christ Jesus to do good works, which God prepared in advance for us to do."*

This confidence isn't about arrogance; it's about trusting that our worth is grounded in God's unchanging love. It's about stepping out in faith, knowing that our identity is secure. This confidence enables us to make choices aligned with God's purposes, rather than bending to the pressures of the world.

David's encounter with Goliath is a powerful example of confidence rooted in God's value. David wasn't the tallest or strongest, but he knew his worth in God. When others doubted him, David said, *"The Lord Who rescued me from the paw of the lion and the paw of the bear will rescue me from the hand of this Philistine"* (1 Samuel 17:37). David's confidence wasn't in himself; it was in the God Who valued and equipped him.

In the same way, when we understand our worth in God, we can face challenges with a confidence that comes from Him. We don't need to rely on our own strength or qualifications. Our confidence is grounded in knowing that God is with us, working through us, and valuing us each step of the way.

Living in confidence of God's value is not just a personal journey; it's a collective experience that shapes our relationships and communities. As we embrace our identity as beloved children of God, we unlock the potential to live joyfully, generously, and authentically. And living confidently in God's value empowers us to extend that same grace to others. When we recognize our worth, we can better appreciate the worth of those around us. It's like hosting a potluck dinner where everyone brings their own unique dish—some might be sweet, some savory, and others a little spicy! Just as we celebrate the diversity of flavors, we can celebrate the diversity of gifts and backgrounds that others bring into our lives. This creates a community where everyone feels valued and included, fostering an environment rich in love and acceptance.

Reflection Questions

- *How does understanding your worth in God affect your confidence in daily life?*

- *What steps can you take to live out your God-given value with boldness?*

Reflection Exercise

Write a list of areas where you struggle with confidence. Next to each one, write a truth about God's love and worth for you. For example: "In my job, I feel insecure about my abilities, but I am God's handiwork, created for a purpose, and I can do all things trough Him." Use this list as a reminder to ground your confidence in God's value, rather than in external validation.

PART 2

NAVIGATING LIFE'S CHALLENGES

Chapter 4

Why Do I Suffer?

The Reality of Suffering

SUFFERING IS AN INESCAPABLE reality of human existence. Whether through personal pain, loss, or witnessing the brokenness of the world, we all face moments of intense struggle. But why does a good and loving God allow suffering? Understanding suffering through a Christian lens not only provides comfort, but also reveals God's greater purpose for our pain.

I remember one night in particular when suffering felt like a mountain pressing down on me. In a matter of one year, I had lost my grandmother, my brother, and my father. It felt like my world was falling apart. Literally. I sat alone in my car in a parking lot, unable to hold back tears anymore. I asked, *Why? Why does life have to hurt like this?* It was a question that hung in the air, heavy and unresolved. It hurt even more when I thought about my mother, who had lost her mother, her son, and husband of over forty years in a matter of months.

As I sat there, my mind went back to a verse I'd read countless times: *"In this world, you will have trouble. But take heart! I have overcome the world"* (John 16:33). The words felt strangely comforting, even if they didn't answer all my questions. They reminded me that suffering wasn't unique to me—it was a part of the human condition. And somehow, knowing that God was aware of this reality, that He saw and understood it, gave me a sense of comfort, even in the pain. The questions remained, and they lingered; but a unique sense of comfort was there.

Suffering is something we all encounter, regardless of who we are or where we come from. The Bible doesn't shy away from this reality; instead, it acknowledges suffering as an inevitable part of life in a fallen world. Genesis 3:17 explains that suffering entered the world as a consequence of sin: *"Cursed is the ground because of you; through painful toil you will eat food from it all the days of your life."* This verse shows that suffering wasn't part of God's original design, but that it came as a result of humanity's choice to stray from Him.

Yet, even in a world marred by suffering, God remains close. He doesn't leave us to navigate pain on our own. In fact, the Bible is filled with God's promises to be with us in our struggles, to offer comfort, and ultimately to restore all things. Knowing that suffering is part of the brokenness of this world helps us make sense of it, even if it doesn't erase the pain. Romans 8:18 says, *"I consider that our present sufferings are not worth comparing with the glory that will be revealed in us."*

The story of Adam and Eve in Genesis 3 shows us how suffering became a part of the human experience. When they chose to disobey God, their relationship with Him and with each other was fractured. This separation led to a world where suffering, pain, and death became realities. Romans 5:12 explains it further: *"Therefore, just as sin entered the world through one man, and death through sin, and in this way death came to all people, because all sinned."* This verse underscores that suffering is not random—it is a symptom of the world's brokenness. Yet, God's presence in our suffering offers us hope. He doesn't abandon us to endure it alone, but promises to be with us, offering strength and comfort. And while free will plays a crucial role in the existence of suffering, it also empowers us to make choices that can lead to healing and redemption.

James 1:2-4 encourages us to *"consider it pure joy"* when we face trials. Really, James? Pure joy? It almost sounds like a misprint! But the idea here is that trials produce perseverance, and perseverance leads to maturity. This is not a call to wear a plastic smile while we're in the thick of it. Instead, it's an invitation to recognize that our struggles can lead to something profoundly good.

You might be wondering, "Why on earth would God allow suffering?" I mean, What purpose does pain serve from a divine perspective? These questions are as old as time, and they have baffled theologians and everyday folks alike. But here's a spicy little nugget: suffering isn't always about punishment or a test of faith. Sometimes, it's a divine invitation to grow in ways we never imagined! Think of it as God's way of saying, "Hey, let's do some deep cleaning in that heart of yours!" Just like a diamond emerges from the pressure of the Earth, our character is sharpened and refined through the challenges we face. So, while we might not enjoy the process, we can be sure that God is at work, shaping us into something beautiful.

The Bible uses the metaphor of a refiner's fire to explain how suffering can serve a transformative purpose in our lives. Understanding the process of refining metals draws parallels to how trials can purify and strengthen our faith. Scriptural references like Malachi 3:2-3 and 1 Peter 1:6-7 delve deeper into the concept of being refined by trials. Our periods of suffering, while challenging, are designed to strip away impurities, leading to a stronger, more genuine faith. Seek God's presence and guidance during their trials, this way you may find meaning and purpose in your suffering, viewing these experiences as opportunities for spiritual growth and closer communion with God.

There are various biblical narratives and teachings that shed light on the role of suffering in refining faith, developing character, and fostering dependence on God. Stories such as Joseph's trials in Egypt and Paul's thorn in the flesh to illustrate how God uses difficult circumstances for good, according to His sovereign plan.

Additionally, suffering can bring us closer to one another, not just to God. I call this concept the fellowship of suffering. There's a unique camaraderie that forms when we share our stories of hardship. It's like a secret club where the only membership requirement is to have experienced a little pain. In our moments of vulnerability, we discover that we're not alone in our struggles—others have walked the same rocky path. And in those shared experiences, we often find the divine presence comforting us, reminding us that we are held in love even in our darkest hours.

There is an important component in the communal aspect of suffering. Shared experiences of pain can create deep bonds among believers and with Christ. Isaiah 53 and Philippians 3:10 provide a foundation for understanding how suffering connects us more intimately to Jesus. But shared trials can also lead to mutual support, empathy, and a stronger collective faith, which underscores the importance of community in the Christian journey.

So, the next time you find yourself asking, "Why me?" take a moment to shift your perspective. Consider how your suffering can be a catalyst for growth, a bridge to deeper connections, and a pathway to divine insights that will illuminate your life's journey.

Reflection Questions

- *How does understanding the origin of suffering affect your perspective on pain?*

- *What does it mean to you that God acknowledges suffering as part of life in this world?*

Reflection Exercise

Take a few moments to reflect on a time when you experienced significant suffering. Write down how that experience affected your faith and your understanding of God. Then, consider how knowing that suffering is a shared human experience can bring comfort and solidarity in times of pain.

The Purpose of Suffering

A friend of mine went through a painful divorce a few years ago, a season that shook him to his core. In the early days, he told me that it felt like everything he'd worked for and dreamed of had been taken from him. The pain was raw, and the future felt uncertain. But over time, he began to see glimpses of growth and resilience in himself that he hadn't seen before. He found himself reaching out to others, offering empathy and support to people going through similar pain.

One day, he shared with me a verse from James 1:2-3: "*Consider it pure joy, my brothers and sisters, whenever you face trials of many kinds, because you know that the testing of your faith produces perseverance.*" He explained that while he would never wish that pain upon himself again, he could see how God was using it to shape him, to deepen his faith, and to enable him to help others. It's not that it was God's will for him and his ex-wife to go through this divorce, or that He had caused it. Far from it. But rather, that even through difficulty and pain, God could use it to help him, and others through him.

While suffering is difficult and often feels purposeless, the Bible teaches that God can use our trials to refine us, strengthen our faith, and draw us closer to Him. Again, I am not suggesting that God causes them; we've established these are a result of sin. But James 1:2-3 speaks directly to this truth, encouraging us to see trials not as pointless suffering, but as opportunities for growth. Now, of course this perspective doesn't make suffering easy, but it certainly gives it meaning.

Pete echoes this idea in 1 Peter 1:6-7 saying, *"In all this you greatly rejoice, though now for a little while you may have had to suffer grief in all kinds of trials. These have come so that the proven genuineness of your faith... may result in praise, glory, and honor when Jesus Christ is revealed."* Here, we see that suffering, while painful and not a part of God's original plan, can still serve a greater purpose in God's overall plan.

Suffering is a universal experience, one that even the most devout Christians can't seem to dodge. From the trials of Job to the heart-wrenching moments of Jesus in Gethsemane, the Bible doesn't shy away from the hard stuff. Instead of viewing suffering as a cruel cosmic joke, we can see it as a divine opportunity—like a heavenly gym membership that promises growth in faith and resilience.

The story of Job (Job 1-2, 38-42) is one of the Bible's most powerful examples of how suffering can serve a purpose beyond our understanding. His story is a profound exploration of human suffering and divine sovereignty. Job was a righteous man who endured incredible suffering—losing his family, his health, and his possessions and wealth, without explanation. Despite the overwhelming pain and confusion, Job clings to his faith in God. In the end, God speaks to Job, revealing His vastness and wisdom, though He doesn't provide a direct answer to Job's suffering.

However, Job's story shows us that even in the midst of unexplainable hardship, God's presence is constant, and His purposes are ultimately good, even if we don't fully understand them in the moment. God's purposes in our trials are often beyond our comprehension. But through his story, we learn that suffering is not something that God causes and also that it is not always a result of wrongdoing. Thankfully, in the end, Job's faith was refined, and God restored him.

So suffering isn't punishment; it's part of our transformative journey. Romans 5:3-5 tells us that suffering produces perseverance, character, and hope. The purpose of suffering is not to leave us broken, but to mold us into the masterpieces we are meant to be. Just as a potter shapes clay, God uses our struggles to refine us, creating vessels of strength and beauty. In this playful dance between suffering and growth, we discover that God's plans are often richer than our own. So, the next time you find yourself wrapped in the trials of life, remember that you're not just surviving—you're being shaped, strengthened, and prepared for the extraordinary journey ahead. Embrace the process, and you might just find that suffering has a purpose after all!

Suffering and the Human Condition

The human experience is marked by suffering, and this reality often leads to confusion and questioning. But to understand suffering, we need to look at the world through the lens of the Bible. When Adam and Eve sinned in the Garden of Eden, sin entered the world, bringing with it suffering and death (Romans 5:12). Humanity's rebellion against God disrupted the original harmony of creation, resulting in a world that now groans under the weight of corruption (Romans 8:22). Suffering, then, is a consequence of living in a fallen world.

Genesis 3:17-19 says, *"Cursed is the ground because of you; through painful toil you will eat food from it all the days of your life. It will produce thorns and thistles for you, and you will eat the plants of the field. By the sweat of your brow, you will eat your food until you return to the ground, since from it you were taken; for dust you are and to dust you will return."*

The fall of Adam and Eve (Genesis 3:1-19) is the origin of all human suffering. Their disobedience led to a cursed ground, toil, pain in childbirth, and ultimately death. Their choice to defy God brought separation from Him, not just spiritually but also in the form of suffering in the physical world. So, suffering is a consequence of sin. The world's brokenness, including natural disasters, illness, and death, is a result of the fall of humanity. God did not create suffering, but it entered the world through sin.

Suffering is universal; no one is exempt from the effects of sin. Whether we experience physical pain, emotional distress, or relational conflict, suffering touches all of us. Understanding that suffering stems from the fall allows us to see the bigger picture. The brokenness of the world is a temporary state, not God's original design. But God has a plan to restore Creation. Though suffering is part of the human condition, for now, God has promised to one day restore all things and eliminate suffering forever.

God doesn't delight in our pain. God is compassionate and loving, and He does not cause suffering for His pleasure. He is present with us in our pain. Nonetheless, suffering has a purpose. While we may not understand it fully, God uses suffering to grow our faith, refine our character, and draw us closer to Him. So, even within this narrative of judgment, God promises hope—He alludes to the coming of Christ, Who would ultimately crush the serpent and defeat sin and death.

And the good news is that Jesus understands our suffering. Jesus Himself experienced pain, betrayal, and death. He is intimately familiar with human suffering and offers comfort because He understands. Remember, suffering is temporary. Our present pain is not the end of the story. God promises that one day, He will wipe away every tear and make all things new (Revelation 21:4).

Romans 8:28 offers us a hopeful promise: *"And we know that in all things God works for the good of those who love Him, who have been called according to His purpose."* Again, while this doesn't mean that suffering is good in itself, it reassures us that God can bring good from our pain, using it to build our character, deepen our relationship with Him, and equip us to help others.

Reflection Questions

- *How have you seen growth or positive change emerge from a season of suffering in your life?*

- *What does it mean to you that God can use even our pain for His purposes?*

Reflection Exercise

Reflect on a time when you faced hardship. Write down any positive changes or growth you experienced as a result of that season. Then, take a moment to thank God for His ability to bring good from our pain, even when we don't fully understand it.

God's Presence in Our Suffering

During this particularly tough season of my life I made reference to above, I also remember feeling deserted. It was as though every prayer I sent up was met with silence, and I began to wonder if God even cared about what my family was going through. One day, while reading Psalms, I came across Psalm 34:18: *"The Lord is close to the brokenhearted and saves those who are crushed in spirit."*

Those words hit me deeply. I realized that even though I couldn't feel it, God's presence was there, right in the middle of our pain. It was a turning point for me—a reminder that God's silence didn't mean His absence. I started to see that, even in our darkest moments, God was closer than we realized, offering comfort and strength.

And this is one of the most comforting truths of Scripture: that God is not distant in our suffering. He is deeply aware of our pain and intimately involved in our lives. The

Bible repeatedly shows us that God is near to the brokenhearted (Psalm 34:18), and His love for us remains steadfast, even in our darkest moments. In fact, it is often in times of suffering that we experience God's presence most powerfully. So while we cannot escape the reality that suffering is a part of our world, we have the hope and assurance provided within Scripture for overcoming and finding purpose in our trials.

When we suffer, it's natural to feel as though God is distant. But Scripture assures us that God is present with us in our pain. Psalm 34:18 promises that *"the Lord is close to the brokenhearted."* This verse reminds us that God is not indifferent to our suffering. He draws near, offering comfort and strength to those who are hurting.

When we read scripture, we find countless stories of people who faced suffering, yet experienced God's presence in profound ways. From Job's lamentations to David's tear-soaked psalms, these figures remind us that it's okay to feel lost and bewildered. They didn't shy away from their emotions; instead, they boldly brought them to God. So, when life feels like a roller coaster with more downs than ups, remember that God isn't just a spectator in our struggles; He's right there in the front row, cheering us on as we navigate the twists and turns.

In fact, one of the most comforting truths is that suffering can lead us to a deeper relationship with God. It's like those moments when your best friend shows up with ice cream after a breakup. Suddenly, those heart-wrenching moments become opportunities for connection. In our suffering, we often discover our need for God in ways we might not have acknowledged before. As we lean on Him, we find that He is not just a distant deity, but a loving Father Who walks beside us, holding our hand through the darkest valleys.

And God's presence during our suffering can lead us to unexpected joy. Picture this: you're having a bad day, and then, out of nowhere, a friend texts you something that makes you laugh. That little burst of joy reminds you that life isn't all doom and gloom. Similarly, God often surprises us with moments of peace, hope, and even laughter amidst our trials. These divine interruptions can shift our focus from our pain to the joy of His presence, reminding us that we are never truly alone.

In Isaiah 43:2, God speaks to His people, saying, *"When you pass through the waters, I will be with you; and when you pass through the rivers, they will not sweep over you."* This verse emphasizes that while we will face difficulties, we will not face them alone. God's presence is a source of strength, carrying us through even the most challenging times.

The story of Shadrach, Meshach, and Abednego in Daniel 3 is a profound illustration of God's presence in the midst of suffering. When these three men refused to bow to an idol, they were thrown into a fiery furnace. Yet, instead of being consumed by the flames, they were protected, and a fourth figure—identified as a possible representation of God, perhaps Jesus pre-incarnate—was seen walking with them in the fire. This story reminds us that God doesn't always remove us from suffering, but that He is with us in it, providing strength and protection.

Paul in 2 Corinthians 12:9-10 further reminds us that God's grace is sufficient, even in our weakness. He writes about a *"thorn in the flesh,"* a form of suffering that God did not remove. Instead, God assured Paul, *"My grace is sufficient for you, for My power is made perfect in weakness."* This passage shows us that God's strength often shines brightest in our most challenging moments.

Hope in the Midst of Suffering

While suffering is an inevitable part of life, the Bible offers us hope that transcends our pain. God promises that our suffering is not without purpose, and that it will ultimately give way to eternal joy and restoration. Through Jesus Christ, we are assured that no matter what trials we face, there is hope for redemption, healing, and peace. The suffering of this present time is not worth comparing to the glory that will be revealed (Romans 8:18). Revelation 21:4 says that *"He will wipe every tear from their eyes. There will be no more death or mourning or crying or pain, for the old order of things has passed away."*

The story of Lazarus' death and resurrection (John 11:1-44) is a powerful testimony to God's compassion and His presence in the midst of our suffering. When Lazarus died, Jesus arrived at the scene and saw Mary and Martha weeping. In response, Jesus wept with them, showing that He shared in their pain. Yet, even in their sorrow, Jesus revealed His power by raising Lazarus from the dead. This story reminds us that God is not only with us in our suffering, but that He also has the power to bring life from death.

God is always near in our times of trouble. God is not indifferent to our pain; He is close to us, offering comfort and strength. As both fully God and fully human, Jesus experienced suffering firsthand. He knows our pain and walks with us through it. And God's comfort empowers us to comfort others. The comfort we receive from Him enables us to extend that same comfort to others who are suffering.

Suffering can refine our character. Like gold in the fire, God uses suffering to refine us, purifying our faith and making us more like Christ. Perseverance through suffering produces hope. As we endure trials, God produces perseverance, character, and ultimately hope in our lives. And God does not waste our pain. While suffering is difficult, it is not wasted. uses our pain for His greater purposes, preparing us for what lies ahead.

So, remember, God can use suffering to grow our character, strengthen our faith, and bring us closer to Him. We must remember that there is hope beyond this temporary life. Suffering is temporary. God promises a future where pain will no longer exist. God works through our pain for good. Even when we don't understand it, God is using our trials for a greater purpose, weaving them into His plan for our lives.

Reflection Questions

- *How has suffering shaped your relationship with God?*

- *When have you felt God's presence during a time of suffering?*

- *How does knowing that God is with you in your pain affect your view of hardship?*

- *How can you use your experiences of suffering to comfort others?*

Reflection Exercise

Take a moment to write a prayer, inviting God into any areas of suffering or hardship you're currently experiencing. Acknowledge His presence with you in this season, and ask for His comfort and strength. Use Psalm 34:18 as a reminder that God is near, even when life feels overwhelming.

Chapter 5

Where Is God in My Pain?

God's Compassion for Our Pain

ONE OF THE MOST challenging aspects of suffering is the feeling of abandonment or the haunting question: "Where is God?" When we face pain and hardship, it can seem as though God is distant, silent, or even absent altogether. Yet, the Bible offers a counter-narrative to this feeling, revealing that God is not only present in our pain, but also intimately involved in our suffering. The psalmist says in Psalm 23:4, *"Even though I walk through the darkest valley, I will fear no evil, for You are with me; Your rod and Your staff, they comfort me."*

I vividly remember sitting in a hospital waiting room once, feeling completely numb. A student of mine was undergoing a difficult surgery, and I was filled with worry and helplessness. The foreign student didn't have anyone in the country, and he didn't even speak English. With my broken Portuguese (or *Portuñol*, rather), I was able to communicate with him and help him. I remember him telling me right before that he was scared. He was in pain, both physically and emotionally, and he just couldn't understand it. Why had this happened to him? I clearly remember I tried to pray as I waited, but the words just wouldn't come. All I could manage were a few silent tears, questioning if God was really there with us in that moment of pain. I remember thinking, *Does He see this? Does He care?*

In the quiet of that crowded waiting room, a verse surfaced in my heart: *"The Lord is close to the brokenhearted and saves those who are crushed in spirit"* (Psalm 34:18). For the first time in hours, I felt a sense of peace. God's presence wasn't going to erase the fear, but it was there with my student, and that made all the difference. God's heart, I realized, also breaks when ours does. He wasn't distant; He was right there, sharing in his pain.

One of the most beautiful aspects of God's character is His compassion. Scripture reveals that God cares deeply about our suffering and that He grieves with us. Psalm 103:13-14 says, *"As a father has compassion on his children, so the Lord has compassion on those who fear Him; for He knows how we are formed, He remembers that we are dust."* This passage paints a picture of a God Who doesn't overlook our pain, but is moved by it, just as a loving parent is moved by their child's struggles.

In times of suffering, it's easy to wonder if God cares. But the Bible repeatedly shows us that God is not indifferent to our pain. He is a God Who draws close, offering comfort and presence when we need it most. Jesus Himself embodies this compassion. In John 11, when Jesus saw Mary and others grieving over the death of their friend Lazarus, He wept. This moment shows us a Savior Who doesn't just see our pain from afar, but enters into it, feeling the weight of our grief and sorrow.

The story of Jesus grieving over Lazarus in John 11 is one of the clearest examples of God's compassion. Although Jesus knew He would raise Lazarus from the dead, He still wept with Mary and Martha. This act of weeping demonstrates that God does not dismiss our pain as insignificant; rather, He shares in it. Jesus' tears show us a God Who isn't removed from human suffering, but intimately involved in it.

The story of Jesus calming the storm (Mark 4:35-41) also serves as a reminder of God's presence in the midst of chaos and fear. The disciples, caught in a fierce storm on the Sea of Galilee, were terrified and felt that Jesus was indifferent to their plight, as He was asleep in the boat. In their desperation, they cried out, "Teacher, don't you care if we drown?" Yet, with a single command, Jesus stilled the storm, revealing that He was always in control, even when they felt abandoned. This story illustrates that God is with us in the "storms" of life, even when it seems like He is silent.

Matthew 11:28 also speaks to God's compassion, where Jesus says, *"Come to Me, all you who are weary and burdened, and I will give you rest."* This invitation reflects a God Who welcomes us to bring our pain to Him, knowing that He cares deeply and offers comfort to the weary.

God is always present, even when we don't feel Him. Our feelings might deceive us, making it seem like God is absent, but His Word assures us that He never leaves us. This means that God's silence is not His absence. Sometimes, God allows us to walk through seasons of silence to deepen our faith and reliance on Him, but He is still actively working behind the scenes. And God is not indifferent to our pain. Just as Jesus wept with Mary and Martha at the death of Lazarus, God shares in our sorrow and is moved by our suffering. So, while we may not understand why we suffer, we can trust that God is in control, and He will ultimately bring good out of our pain. Oh, and by the way, although there were complications, eventually, everything turned out okay for my student.

In the midst of all the twists and turns, one thing remains wonderfully clear: God's compassion for our pain is as deep as the ocean and as steady as the sunrise. Imagine a heavenly parent watching over us, ready to scoop us up in a warm embrace every time we stumble. The good news is that we don't have to navigate life's challenges alone; our Creator is right there with us, holding our hearts in His hands.

When we face pain, it's easy to feel isolated or forgotten. Yet, God's compassion invites us to lean into our struggles rather than shy away from them. Think about it: even Jesus, during His earthly ministry, didn't shy away from pain. From mourning the loss of friends to feeling the weight of the world on His shoulders, He walked through the valley of suffering with us in mind. His empathy isn't just a comforting thought; it serves as an invitation for us to bring our burdens before Him. *"Come to me, all you who are weary and burdened, and I will give you rest"* (Matthew 11:28) isn't just a nice saying; it's a divine promise wrapped in love that comes out of empathetic compassion and total understanding.

But God's compassion doesn't stop at mere empathy; it flows into action. Think of the countless stories in the Bible where God intervened in the lives of those in pain. From the woman at the well feeling the weight of her past to the blind man who yearned for sight, God didn't just acknowledge their struggles. He stepped in, bringing healing, hope, and restoration. Our own experiences of pain are no less significant in the grand tapestry of His love. Every tear we shed is noticed, every heartache felt. When we invite God into our pain, we open the door for miraculous transformations to take place.

Thankfully, the Bible demonstrates over and over that it is appropriate to incorporate lament into our prayer life. Multiple characters, including Jesus, expressed their grief and questions to God, and by doing so, they found solace in God's presence. Even when at times the answer was silence. Lament is a valid, necessary form of prayer that can lead to comfort and clarity in times of suffering. The Book of Lamentations and the psalms of lament articulate deep anguish, while also affirming trust in God. There is a therapeutic and relational aspect of lament, as it allows for a genuine expression of pain and fosters a deeper relationship with God.

So, when the waves of life threaten to pull you under, remember that God's compassion is a lifeline. It's a reminder that you're not just a face in a crowd, but a cherished child of the Creator, worthy of comfort and love, and who can came to Him with lamentations. Embrace the idea that your pain is not a sign of abandonment, but an opportunity for divine connection. As you navigate life's challenges, hold onto the truth that God is there, ready to catch you when you fall, to lift you when you're weary, and to remind you, in the most playful and loving way, that you are never alone.

Reflection Questions

- *Have there been times in your life when you felt abandoned by God? How did you respond?*

- *What are some ways you've seen God working behind the scenes in your suffering, even if you didn't realize it at the time?*

- *How does knowing that God grieves with you change your perspective on suffering?*

Reflection Exercise

Spend a few moments reflecting on a time when you felt God's compassion in the midst of pain. Write down what you felt, what verses or words gave you comfort, and how this experience shaped your understanding of God's character. If you're currently going through a hard season, pray and invite God's compassionate presence into your situation, asking Him to help you feel His comfort and closeness.

God's Sovereignty in Pain

A couple of years ago, I spoke with an older church lady who had gone through a long period of disappointment and unanswered prayers. She had faced setback after setback, and each one made her question why God would allow her to go through so much pain. As we were talking, she shared a verse from Isaiah that had recently given her peace: *"For My thoughts are not your thoughts, neither are your ways My ways, declares the Lord. As the heavens are higher than the Earth, so are My ways higher than your ways and My thoughts than your thoughts"* (Isaiah 55:8-9).

In that moment, she explained, she realized that God's understanding was beyond her own. She began to see that while she didn't understand why she was facing these hardships, she could trust that God had a purpose. Her pain didn't suddenly disappear, but she felt comforted by the idea that God was in control, even if she couldn't see the full picture.

I truly believe that one of the hardest parts of suffering is not understanding why it happens. Yet, the Bible teaches us that God is sovereign, meaning He is in control and has a purpose, even when we can't see it. Again, I am not suggesting that suffering comes from God. Far from it. God is good all the time! And yet, He can use that suffering for good in our lives. Isaiah 55:8-9 reminds us that God's thoughts and ways are higher than ours. This also doesn't mean that suffering is easy to accept, but it does mean that we can trust that God's purposes are beyond our understanding.

Romans 8:28 offers hope in the midst of pain, saying, *"And we know that in all things God works for the good of those who love Him, who have been called according to His purpose."* This verse doesn't suggest that everything we go through is good; rather, it assures us that God can bring good out of even the most difficult situations. Trusting in God's sovereignty means resting in the knowledge that He sees the bigger picture and is working for our ultimate good.

Pain often brings with it the feeling of being abandoned by God. When we are hurting, it can seem like our prayers are going unanswered and that God has turned His back on us. This feeling is not new. Throughout the Bible, even some of the most faithful figures struggled with this sense of abandonment. King David, a man after God's own heart, frequently cried out in the Psalms, asking why God seemed far away in his time of need (Psalm 13:1-2; 22:1-2). Yet, through it all, David ultimately trusted that God was near, even when he couldn't perceive His presence.

David's lament in Psalm 22, often called the "Psalm of the Cross," is a poignant example of feeling forsaken by God. David expresses deep anguish, feeling as though God has abandoned him in his time of greatest need. Yet, the psalm doesn't end in despair. David transitions from his complaint to a declaration of trust in God's faithfulness, knowing that God will ultimately deliver him. This psalm foreshadows Christ's own cry of abandonment on the cross (Matthew 27:46), reminding us that even in our most painful moments, God is with us.

From this, we learn that it's okay to express your pain to God. David's honest cries show us that it's natural to wrestle with feelings of abandonment, and God invites us to bring our raw emotions to Him. After all, God is faithful, even when we don't see it. Like David, we can move from lament to trust, knowing that God's faithfulness transcends our circumstances. And Jesus understands our abandonment. Jesus, in His moment of greatest agony on the cross, felt forsaken by the Father. He knows what it's like to feel abandoned and offers us His empathy.

But, while we may not always see God's hand in our suffering, the Bible assures us that He is at work, even when He seems hidden. Like a tapestry being woven from the back, our lives can appear chaotic and tangled, but God is creating something beautiful from our pain. Joseph's story in Genesis is a powerful illustration of this, and it clearly demonstrates God's sovereignty. Sold into slavery by his own brothers, unjustly imprisoned, and forgotten, Joseph endured years of hardship. He had every reason to believe that God had abandoned him.

Yet, years later, Joseph recognized that God had been working through his suffering all along to accomplish a greater purpose. Of course God never wanted this for him. In fact, the life of Joseph is a remarkable example of God's hidden work in suffering. As the story unfolds, it becomes clear that God was using these painful experiences to position Joseph in a place of influence where he could save his family and an entire nation from famine. What appeared to be abandonment was, in fact, divine orchestration. In Genesis 50:20, Joseph tells his brothers, *"You intended to harm me, but God intended it for good to accomplish what is now being done, the saving of many lives."* This isn't just a fairy tale ending; it's a powerful reminder that God can turn our struggles into stepping stones for something beautiful. His sovereignty doesn't merely allow pain; it redeems it, transforming our mess into a masterpiece.

And this verse reflects a profound truth: even in our darkest moments, God's sovereign hand is at work, bringing good from our suffering. The devil might bring you suffering, but God is faithful to use it for your benefit. Stay strong through His promises and remain faithful and trust Him through it all.

In the same way, God can redeem our suffering. Like Joseph, we may not see it at the time, but God is working behind the scenes to bring good out of our pain. His plans are much bigger and better than our understanding. We may never fully comprehend why we suffer, but we can trust that God's ways are higher than ours and that He is weaving together a greater story. Our suffering can have a purpose beyond ourselves. Joseph's suffering led to the saving of many lives. And in the same way, God can use our pain to impact others and further His kingdom.

God's sovereignty in pain might seem like a puzzling puzzle piece in the grand picture of our lives. Imagine sitting at a table with your favorite jigsaw, and there's that one piece that just doesn't seem to fit anywhere. Yet, when we step back and look at the entire landscape, it becomes clear that every piece, including the tricky ones, plays a role. The Bible invites us to see pain not as a standalone event but as a part of a masterful design crafted by a divine artist. So, grab your magnifying glass as we explore how God's sovereignty reigns even in our most challenging moments.

Pain and suffering are like those unwelcomed guest that shows up at the party and refuse to leave. However, it's in these sticky situations that we often discover a profound truth: God's presence is most palpable when we are at our weakest. Paul's thorn in the flesh is a classic example. Instead of removing it, God told him, "*My grace is sufficient for you, for my power is made perfect in weakness.*" It's like God is saying, "Hey, I know this hurts, but guess what? You're never alone in this." That's where the magic happens—when we lean into that divine strength.

Reflection Questions

- *What does it mean to you that God is sovereign, even in pain?*

- *How can trusting God's higher purposes help you endure difficult times?*

Reflection Exercise

Write down an area of pain or disappointment in your life. Reflect on how God's sovereignty and faithfulness might bring comfort, even if the situation remains unresolved or things don't go your way in the end. Then, write a prayer, surrendering this area to God's wisdom and asking for the faith to trust in His greater plan, even when it's difficult to understand.

God's Healing Through Pain

Years ago, when I worked at a Christian university, I met a man at work who was brought to share his story. He had gone through a life-changing accident. Thanks for a drunk driver, he had lost his mobility and had to relearn basic tasks. But worst of all, he had lost his toddler son. At first, he was overwhelmed by anger and frustration, feeling as though life had robbed him of everything he valued. But as time went on, as he shared, he experienced a transformation. Through his pain, he found a deeper relationship with God and a purpose he hadn't seen before. And though the pain and many questions remained, he became a source of encouragement for others facing similar challenges.

He explained that while his physical circumstances had changed, his heart had been healed in ways he never imagined. His accident, he said, had become a catalyst for a new chapter, one where God used his pain to bring light and hope to others. Eventually he learned to forgive the young man that had taken everything from him. But he still cried at night and continued to wrestle with God, like Jacob that one night.

While having a devotional during a meeting with some of us workers, the man read Isaiah 61:1 to us, where God promises to *"bind up the brokenhearted, to proclaim freedom for the captives and release from darkness for the prisoners."*

God's healing often goes beyond the physical; He is a healer of hearts and minds. While we may hope for our pain to disappear, sometimes God uses our hardships to bring about deeper transformation in our lives. Psalm 147:3 says, *"He heals the brokenhearted and binds up their wounds."* This verse reminds us that God's healing is holistic, addressing not only our physical needs, but also our emotional and spiritual wounds.

In 2 Corinthians 4:16-17, Paul writes, *"Therefore we do not lose heart. Though outwardly we are wasting away, yet inwardly we are being renewed day by day. For our light and momentary troubles are achieving for us an eternal glory that far outweighs them all."* This passage offers hope that even when we endure pain, God is at work, renewing and strengthening us from within.

The story of the woman with the issue of blood in Luke 8:43-48 is a powerful example of God's healing power. After twelve years of suffering and unsuccessful treatments, she reached out to touch Jesus' cloak, and she was instantly healed. Her story illustrates that Jesus not only heals physical ailments, but also restores dignity and faith. Jesus touch brings transformation. When Jesus speaks to her, calling her "Daughter," He affirms her worth and identity, showing that His healing encompasses both body and soul.

And just as diamonds are forged under pressure, our faith grows stronger through trials and tribulations. Pain can be a powerful catalyst for transformation, leading us to greater depths in our relationship with God and allowing us to reflect His light in a world that desperately needs it. So, the next time you find yourself in the midst of pain, remember: you're not just surviving; you're being crafted into something extraordinary. Trust in the process, lean into the healing, and watch how God turns those painful moments into stepping stones toward a brighter future.

Jesus Is Present In the Ordinary

While we may often look for miraculous signs of God's presence in our suffering, the truth is that God is with us in the ordinary, everyday moments of life. Sometimes, His presence is found in the comfort of a friend, the beauty of creation, or the peace that surpasses understanding. Recognizing God's presence in these small, everyday ways can help us feel less alone in our pain and more aware of His constant companionship. As Matthew 28:20 says, *"And surely I am with you always, to the very end of the age."*

The story of Elijah in 1 Kings 19:11-13 shows how God's presence is not always found in the loud, dramatic moments but often in the quiet, stillness. After fleeing from Queen Jezebel, Elijah is exhausted and afraid. He expects to hear from God through a powerful wind, an earthquake, or a fire. Yet, God speaks to Elijah in a gentle whisper, reminding him that He is present, even in the quiet, everyday moments.

This lets us know that God is also present in the ordinary. While we may expect grand displays of God's presence, He often speaks to us in the quiet, ordinary moments of life. We need to slow down to hear His voice. And like Elijah, we may need to quiet our hearts and minds to perceive God's presence in our lives. God also sometimes uses others to comfort us. Often, God's presence is experienced through the people He places in our lives to offer support, encouragement, and love during our suffering.

Jesus Understands Our Pain

One of the greatest promises of the Bible is that God is with us in our suffering. Even when we do not see or feel Him, God is present, walking with us through every trial. His presence is not always dramatic or visible, but it is always there. We must learn to recognize His presence, even in the depths of our pain. That is why Hebrews 13:5 reminds us that, *"Never will I leave you; never will I forsake you."*

One of the most comforting truths of Christianity is that we serve a God Who understands our pain because He has experienced it Himself (Isaiah 53:3; Hebrews 4:15). Jesus, the Son of God, entered into human suffering in the most profound way through His life and death on the cross. In becoming fully human, He experienced every form of pain—physical, emotional, and spiritual.

The crucifixion of Jesus is the ultimate example of God entering into human suffering. As Jesus hung on the cross, bearing the weight of the world's sin, He cried out, *"My God, my God, why have you forsaken me?"* (Matthew 27:46). In this moment, Jesus experienced the full depth of human pain and abandonment. Yet, through His suffering and death, He made a way for us to be reconciled to God. Jesus' suffering assures us that He understands our pain and stands with us in our darkest moments.

Jesus experienced the full depth of human suffering. He knows what it is like to suffer deeply. And because Jesus suffered, He can empathize with us and offer comfort in our struggles. And His victory over suffering gives us hope. Jesus' resurrection assures us that suffering does not have the final word. His victory over sin, over pain, over suffering, and over death gives us hope for our own redemption.

So, never forget that while we may not always have clear answers to the question of where God is during our trials, we can trust in His love, His empathy, and His promise to never leave us, even when the road is hard.

We live in a reality that is full of pain and loss, and we all navigate our own valleys. Thankfully, the Bible provided an uplifting perspective on moving beyond suffering towards hope and healing. While the Bible provides opportunities for lamentation, it also shifts our focus to the promises of restoration and peace found in passages such as Psalm 23 and Revelation 21:4.

God's presence and promises serve as an anchor in the midst of trials, and in Jesus, our mindsets can transition from despair to hope. In Him we find healing and comfort. So, while suffering is a part of life, it is not the end of the story—hope and healing await on the other side of pain. Seeking God through prayer, Bible study, engaging with supportive communities, and embracing the lessons learned from suffering can help us get out of the dark valleys.

As believers, we are called to maintain faith in the face of adversity, grounded in the biblical teachings of perseverance and trust. Daniel in the lions' den or Paul's numerous hardships. These and many other stories serve as tangible illustrations of how faith can be actively practiced and lived out, even under extreme pressure. I encourage you to reflect on your own experiences of suffering through the lens of these biblical truths. Consider how your trials might be shaping you for a greater purpose.

Reflection Questions

- *Have you ever felt like God was absent during a time of suffering? How did you respond?*

- *How does knowing that Jesus understands your pain change the way you view your suffering?*

- *Have you experienced healing that went beyond physical circumstances? How did it change you?*

- *What areas of your life could benefit from God's transformative healing?*

Reflection Exercise

Think of an area in your life where you've experienced pain, whether physical, emotional, or spiritual. Write down how God has used, or perhaps how He could possibly use this area to bring about healing or growth, either for yourself or for others. Then, pray, asking God to continue working through your pain, transforming it into a source of strength and renewal. As you do this, remember that life might, and most likely will bring problems and pain, but that life with God is always better, and going through this pain with Him by your side you can endure anything.

Chapter 6

How Do I Find Peace?

The Peace of God

THERE WAS A RECENT time in my life when peace and rest felt like a distant memory. I was juggling endless work deadlines, family responsibilities, church responsibilities, financial stressors, possible political upheaval, and the constant buzz of social media, which always seemed to remind me of all the ways I was "falling short." No matter what I did, I couldn't quiet my mind or shake the feeling of being overwhelmed. One night, after yet another restless day, I opened my Bible app on my phone and I came across a verse I'd heard many times but never fully appreciated: "*And the peace of God, which transcends all understanding, will guard your hearts and your minds in Christ Jesus*" (Philippians 4:7).

I read it over and over, letting the words settle in. It struck me that this peace wasn't something I could find by clearing my schedule or reaching some perfect version of myself. It was a gift from God, one that didn't depend on my circumstances. That night, I prayed for the peace of God to fill my heart, and as I surrendered my worries, I felt a stillness I hadn't experienced in a long time.

The peace of God is a unique kind of peace, one that "*transcends all understanding*." It doesn't rely on the absence of problems, but comes from trusting in God's presence in the midst of them. Philippians 4:6-7 tells us to "*not be anxious about anything, but in every situation, by prayer and petition, with thanksgiving, present your requests to God.*" This verse gives us a roadmap to peace: we're invited to bring our worries to God, release them into His hands, and receive a peace that guards our hearts and minds.

This peace isn't based on having all the answers or being in control. Instead, it's rooted in the assurance that God is with us, that He loves us, and that He's working in our lives even when we don't understand His ways. It's a peace that shifts our focus from our circumstances to the One Who holds them all.

The quest for peace is one of humanity's deepest desires, especially in the face of life's challenges. We've all had this question: In a world filled with turmoil, how can we find true peace? True peace, according to the Bible, is not merely the absence of conflict or trouble, but a deep, abiding sense of wholeness and security that comes from God. This peace is something that surpasses all human understanding and cannot be shaken by external circumstances. In John 14:27, Jesus says, *"Peace I leave with you; my peace I give you. I do not give to you as the world gives. Do not let your hearts be troubled and do not be afraid."*

In the Gospel of Mark, we see a vivid picture of this peace in the story of Jesus calming the storm (Mark 4:35-41). While the disciples panicked as the waves crashed around them, Jesus slept peacefully in the boat. When they woke Him, terrified, He simply rebuked the wind and calmed the sea, asking them, *"Why are you so afraid? Do you still have no faith?"* Jesus' calm in the midst of chaos reminds us that peace isn't about having a life free from storms. It's about trusting the One Who has power over them. This story illustrates that even in life's most turbulent moments, God's peace is available to us, and He has the power to calm the storms in our hearts.

Isaiah 26:3 also speaks of God's peace, saying, *"You will keep in perfect peace those whose minds are steadfast, because they trust in You."* This verse shows that peace comes not from our ability to control life, but from placing our trust in God.

God's peace is available to all believers. Through Christ, we can experience a deep, abiding peace that goes beyond human understanding. True peace is not dependent on circumstances; God's peace remains with us even in the most chaotic times, just as Jesus calmed the storm for His disciples. Perfect peace comes when we trust in God's sovereignty and place our anxieties in His hands.

And peace is contagious. When we embody the peace of God, we become beacons of light for those around us. It's like being the friend who always carries snacks to the movie theater—everyone wants to be near you! By sharing our experiences of God's peace, we encourage others to seek it for themselves.

Reflection Questions

- *How do you typically respond to stressful or chaotic situations? Do you seek God's peace, or do you try to handle things on your own?*

- *What steps can you take to pursue peace with others, especially in relationships where there is conflict or tension?*

- *How does the idea of peace that transcends understanding change your view of your current challenges?*

- *What steps can you take to trust God more deeply in areas where you're seeking peace?*

Reflection Exercise

Take a few minutes to write down your current worries or anxieties. Next to each one, write a short prayer, asking God to bring peace into that specific area. As you do this, read Philippians 4:7 and pray for God's peace to guard your heart and mind, trusting that He is with you in each circumstance.

Peace with Others and Ourselves

God calls us not only to experience peace within ourselves, but also to pursue peace with others. In a world filled with conflict and division, the Bible challenges us to be peacemakers, extending grace and forgiveness to others as we have received it from God. Ephesians 4:3 encourages us to *"make every effort to keep the unity of the Spirit through the bond of peace."*

In Genesis 13, we see the story of Abram and Lot. As their families and herds grew, tension arose between their herdsmen over land and resources. Rather than allowing the conflict to escalate, Abram took the initiative to make peace by offering Lot the first choice of land. This act of humility and generosity helped preserve their relationship and set an example of how we can pursue peace, even when it means making personal sacrifices.

Pursuing peace requires effort. Living at peace with others doesn't happen naturally; it takes intentional effort, humility, and a willingness to forgive. Peacemaking is a reflection of God's nature, and as children of God, we are called to be peacemakers, reflecting His grace and love in our relationships. Sometimes, pursuing peace means sacrificing pride and setting aside our own preferences or desires, as Abram did, for the sake of harmony.

I once heard a story about two neighbors who, for years, had barely spoken to each other. It all started with a small disagreement over a fence, which grew into years of bitterness and silence. One day, one of them decided to break the silence. He walked over to his neighbor's house, knocked on the door, and said, "I'm sorry for letting something so small come between us. Can we put it behind us?"

The other neighbor was surprised but deeply moved. That simple act of humility and forgiveness transformed their relationship, and they became close friends. Their story reminded me of something Jesus said: *"Blessed are the peacemakers, for they will be called children of God"* (Matthew 5:9). Being a peacemaker isn't about winning arguments or being right; it's about choosing love and forgiveness over pride.

Jesus calls His followers to be peacemakers, people who actively seek reconciliation and harmony. In Romans 12:18, Paul encourages us, *"If it is possible, as far as it depends on you, live at peace with everyone."* This verse acknowledges that peace isn't always easy to achieve, but it challenges us to do our part in pursuing it.

You may have noticed that some people come into our lives like a refreshing breeze, while others are more like a gusty wind who flings open the windows of our souls. Biblical wisdom reminds us that peace isn't merely the absence of conflict; it's the active pursuit of understanding, compassion, and love. Romans 12:18 nudges us to *"live at peace with everyone."* It's as if God is giving us the ultimate relationship advice: "Do your part, even if it means stepping on a few toes." And let's be honest, sometimes those toes are our own!

The secret ingredient in the recipe for peace with others is forgiveness. Picture it as a magical elixir that transforms bitterness into sweetness. When we forgive, we release ourselves from the shackles of resentment and open the door to healing. Ephesians 4:32 encourages us to be kind and compassionate, forgiving each other just as Christ forgave us.

So, forgiveness is this key component of peace with others. Colossians 3:13 reminds us, *"Bear with each other and forgive one another if any of you has a grievance against someone. Forgive as the Lord forgave you."* Forgiving others doesn't mean ignoring the hurt; it means choosing to let go of bitterness and entrusting justice to God. When we do this, we reflect God's love and bring His peace into our relationships.

Joseph's story in Genesis is a powerful example of peace and forgiveness. After being sold into slavery by his own brothers, Joseph endured years of hardship. Yet, when he finally had the power to punish them, he chose forgiveness instead. In Genesis 50:19-21, Joseph says to his brothers, *"Don't be afraid. Am I in the place of God? You intended to harm me, but God intended it for good."* Joseph's willingness to forgive brought peace to his family and demonstrated God's redemptive power.

Forgiveness allows us to break the cycle of hurt and resentment, opening the door to reconciliation. By choosing to forgive, we become conduits of God's peace, bringing healing to broken relationships. May you truly be an instrument of peace.

In our quest for peace, it's also essential to embrace the beauty of diversity. Just as a symphony requires different instruments to create a harmonious sound, our relationships thrive on a variety of perspectives. Each person brings a unique melody to the table, and when we listen and appreciate these differences, we create a richer, more vibrant community. Galatians 3:28 reminds us that in Christ, we are all one, transcending race, gender, and background. So, let's celebrate our differences with open arms and maybe even a dance party or two!

Forgiveness also plays a crucial role in achieving peace with ourselves. It's easy to hold onto grudges—especially against ourselves for past missteps. But here's the scoop: God's grace is bigger than our blunders! In Colossians 3:13, we're called to forgive as the Lord forgave us. Imagine carrying a heavy backpack filled with rocks of regret and shame; forgiveness is the key that unlocks that burden. As you let go of past mistakes, you create space for joy, healing, and the beautiful peace that comes from knowing you are forgiven.

Ultimately, peace with others and with ourselves is a journey, not a destination. It's about waking up each day with the intention to spread love, kindness, and understanding. It's about choosing joy over conflict and laughter over frustration. And when the storms of life try to shake our foundations, we can lean on God's wisdom to guide us through. So, let's embrace this divine adventure, hand in hand, as we navigate the delightful and sometimes messy gift of relationships, knowing that we are all beautifully imperfect beings learning to dance together in the light of God's love.

Reflection Questions

- *Is there anyone in your life with whom you need to make peace? How might forgiveness play a role in restoring that relationship?*

- *How can you become a peacemaker in your community, family, or workplace?*

Reflection Exercise

Think of a relationship in your life where there is tension or unresolved conflict. Write down one action you can take to seek peace in that relationship—whether it's offering forgiveness, reaching out, or praying for the other person. Ask God to help you become a peacemaker, reflecting His love and grace.

Finding Peace in God's Promises

One of the most powerful lessons on peace I ever received came from my grandmother. She had been through a lot in her life—loss of a husband with four babies, loss of a teenage son, illness, financial hardship—but I never saw her without a calm smile. Once, when I was a teenager, I asked her how she stayed so peaceful. She looked at me, smiled, and said, "I just know that God is with me, no matter what happens." I was surprised with her answer, as at the time she was Roman Catholic and didn't believe or worship as I did. But her words stayed with me, and over the years, I saw her live out that peace in every season.

Ever since then, I held on to verses like Isaiah 41:10, where God says, *"Do not fear, for I am with you; do not be dismayed, for I am your God. I will strengthen you and help you; I will uphold you with My righteous right hand."* If anything, her life taught me that true peace comes from believing God's promises, trusting that He is faithful to keep them.

God's promises are a source of unshakeable peace. When we trust in His Word, we find peace that goes beyond our circumstances. Isaiah 41:10 reassures us that God is with us, offering strength and support when we need it most. This promise of His presence and help is a foundation we can stand on, even when life feels unstable.

In John 14:27, Jesus offers His followers peace, saying, *"Peace I leave with you; My peace I give you. I do not give to you as the world gives. Do not let your hearts be troubled and do not be afraid."* The peace Jesus gives is not temporary or superficial; it is a lasting peace that flows from His unchanging nature and faithful love.

God's peace is greater than our circumstances: Even when the world around us is falling apart, God offers us a peace that transcends our understanding. Peace is not merely a state of mind; it is a gift from God, made possible through Christ, and available to all who seek Him. And sure, finding peace in the midst of global crises, personal tragedies, and uncertainties can seem impossible. However, the Bible reassures us that God's peace is available even in the darkest and most difficult times. Psalm 46:1-2 says that "*God is our refuge and strength, an ever-present help in trouble. Therefore we will not fear, though the earth give way and the mountains fall into the heart of the sea.*"

The story of the Israelites in the wilderness is an example of finding peace in God's promises. Despite facing hunger, thirst, and uncertainty, God provided for them each step of the way, guiding them with a pillar of cloud by day and a pillar of fire by night (Exodus 13:21-22). His presence was a constant reminder that He was with them and would fulfill His promise to lead them to the Promised Land. This same God Who led the Israelites through the wilderness leads us today. When we hold onto His promises, we can find peace even in the wilderness seasons of life, knowing that He will never leave us or forsake us.

Finding Peace by Surrendering and In Community

While it is important to have a strong faith foundation to withstand life's storms, in the end, it's really not about us. Anchoring in God provides a unique ability to offer deep, enduring serenity. When facing a storm, we can only find peace by seeking God's presence in the midst of chaos. But let's be honest, as humans, we have a natural desire for control. And when we are facing a storm, we try to relay on ourselves in order to try and control the situation. Unfortunately, this often only exacerbates the chaos and turmoil we experience. This is why surrendering control is a prerequisite for finding peace. We've all heard the phrase 'let go and let God in.' Surrendering our full lives, including our desire for control, to God leads to peace. We must surrender and anchor in Him.

Another way to find peace amid a storm is in nurturing community. Fostering connections within a Christian community can significantly bolster one's ability to find peace in turbulent times. Scripture clearly states that the Christian community should be a haven of peace in the midst of chaos. The Early Church is a great example for the basis of true fellowship and community. They emphasized providing support, strength, and encouragement to each other in times of need. So engaging with a faith community can also serve as an anchor. That is why there are benefits in communal prayer, shared worship, and mutual support. There is a transformative power in prayer and praise for silencing life's storms. But it is much more powerful when done with fellow believers.

Reflection Questions

- *What promises of God bring you peace during difficult times?*

- *How can holding onto God's promises help you face challenges with a sense of calm and assurance?*

Reflection Exercise

Write down three of God's promises that resonate with you, especially in seasons of difficulty. Next to each one, write a short prayer, thanking God for His faithfulness and asking Him to help you trust in these promises. Keep these promises somewhere visible as a reminder of the peace that comes from trusting in God's Word.

PART 3

TRUSTING GOD IN UNCERTAINTY

Chapter 7

Trusting God in Uncertainty

The Nature of Trust

Years ago, I faced a decision that would change the course of my life, and also that of my family's. I felt a sense of calling to leave my comfortable job and pursue something that aligned more closely with my purpose. But the uncertainty of leaving the security of a regular paycheck and a steady routine filled me with doubt. I had to go back to school, and with a family, this would create financial burdens, as we would have to go back in debt. It also meant moving and leaving a community where we were loved and appreciated. There were just very many uncertainties. What if it didn't work out? What if the plan failed? My wife fully supported me, but I still struggled with whether I could truly trust God with such a big leap.

One day, while reading, I came across Proverbs 3:5-6: "*Trust in the Lord with all your heart and lean not on your own understanding; in all your ways submit to Him, and He will make your paths straight.*" The verse struck me as both comforting and challenging. Trusting God with "*all my heart*" meant letting go of my need for control and relying on Him completely. I took a deep breath and prayed, choosing to take the step, trusting that God would guide me through the unknown.

Trust is the cornerstone of faith, and trusting God means relying on His wisdom and guidance, even when we don't have all the answers. It means having belief in God's promises, reliance on His character, and confidence in His plans. Proverbs 3:5-6 teaches us that genuine trust requires surrendering our need for control, allowing God to lead us on a path that may not always make sense to us. This isn't easy, especially in a world that values independence and self-sufficiency. But biblical trust goes beyond just believing in God's existence—it means depending on Him fully, acknowledging that His ways are higher than ours.

Psalm 56:3-4 echoes this sentiment, saying, *"When I am afraid, I put my trust in you. In God, Whose word I praise—in God I trust and am not afraid."* Trusting God doesn't mean that fear or doubt will disappear, but it does mean choosing faith over fear. Trust anchors us, allowing us to move forward with peace and confidence, even when we're unsure of what lies ahead.

God is always faithful, even when we cannot see the full picture, and His plans are always for our good. However, trusting God is usually easy when life is predictable, but it becomes challenging in times of uncertainty. Trust in God transcends understanding and brings stability in the midst of uncertainty. But biblical trust means more than just a hopeful expectation—it's a deep-rooted confidence in God's faithfulness, even when circumstances don't make sense. Often, our understanding is limited, but God's wisdom is infinite.

Abraham's journey (Genesis 12:1-4) is a powerful example of trust in action. His story is a remarkable example of trusting God beyond understanding. When God called Abraham to leave his homeland and go to a place he'd never seen, Abraham didn't have all the details—he only had God's promise. Hebrews 11:8-10 tells us that Abraham *"obeyed and went, even though he did not know where he was going."* His willingness to step into the unknown, relying on God's promise, is a profound demonstration of trust.

Abraham's journey teaches us that trusting God often means stepping forward in faith, believing that He is faithful to fulfill His promises. His trust led him to become the father of faith, showing us that trusting God often requires stepping out in faith without knowing all the details.

God's wisdom is greater than ours, and we can trust Him because His thoughts and ways are far beyond our understanding, even when we can't see how things will work out. Trusting God requires full surrender. It means letting go of the need to control every aspect of our lives and yielding to His greater plan. Fear and trust can coexist. Just as Abraham moved forward even when uncertainty loomed, we can have moments of fear while still choosing to trust God. In the end, God honors faithful trust. And when we step out in faith, God is faithful to lead us and fulfill His promises, as He did with Abraham. So, uncertainty is an opportunity for growth. Times of uncertainty deepen our faith and reliance on God, refining us for His purposes. When we place our trust in God, we can experience peace and confidence, even in the most uncertain of times.

Imagine trust as a bridge connecting us to God's promises. Just as we wouldn't step onto a rickety bridge, we must evaluate the sturdiness of our faith. Scripture is packed with stories of trust, from Abraham's leap of faith to the steadfastness of Job in his trials. Each tale offers nuggets of wisdom reminding us that trust isn't about having all the answers; it's about believing in God's character and His unwavering love for us. When we embrace this divine trust, we build a solid foundation that can withstand life's tempests.

Yet, trust can feel a bit like a game of hide and seek. Just when we think we've got a grasp on it, uncertainties pop up like mischievous children, making us question our faith. It's easy to trust when everything is going smoothly, but what about those stormy seasons? This is where biblical wisdom shines through. Jesus invites us to cast our cares upon Him (1 Peter 5:7), reminding us that trust isn't the absence of fear, but the presence of faith amid it. Our struggles don't disqualify us from trusting; they can actually deepen our reliance on God.

Now, let's not forget the role trust plays in our relationships with others. It's like a dance—sometimes we lead, sometimes we follow, but the rhythm relies on mutual confidence. As Christians, we are called to trust and be trustworthy, reflecting the love of Christ in our interactions. Proverbs 3:5-6 encourages us to trust in the Lord with all our hearts and lean not on our own understanding. This doesn't just apply to our relationship with God, but also with fellow believers. When we practice trust, we create a safe space for vulnerability and connection, fostering a community built on love and support.

In our journey to deepen our understanding of trust, let's remember that it's a lifelong adventure. Just as we grow in our faith, our ability to trust evolves, shaped by our experiences and the lessons God teaches us. Embracing trust means stepping into the unknown with a heart full of hope, knowing that God is orchestrating a beautiful symphony even in our most chaotic moments. As we navigate life's challenges, let's hold onto the truth that trust is not just a destination; it's a way of life, leading us closer to God and to one another. So, let's take a deep breath, open our hearts, and dance our way through this journey of trust, hand in hand with our Creator.

Reflection Questions

- *What areas of your life are hardest to surrender to God's guidance?*

- *What practical steps can you take this week to grow your trust in God, especially in uncertain times?*

- *How can Abraham's example of trust inspire you to take steps of faith in uncertain situations?*

Reflection Exercise

Take a few moments to identify an area in your life where you struggle with uncertainty. Write down what it would look like to trust God in this area, even without having all the answers. Then, pray, asking God for the courage to step forward in faith, trusting that He will guide you and make your path straight.

Challenges to Trusting God

It is important to recognize the triggers that often lead to doubt, such as personal failures, unexpected tragedies, or unanswered prayers. A friend of mine had dreamed for years about a certain career path, believing that it was God's calling for him. But time after time, doors closed, and he found himself discouraged and questioning God's plan. "I just don't understand," he told me one day. "I thought God wanted this for me. Why isn't it happening?"

As we talked, I shared a verse that had brought me comfort countless times, Jeremiah 29:11: "*For I know the plans I have for you... plans to prosper you and not to harm you, plans to give you hope and a future.*" Slowly, he began to realize that trusting God didn't mean understanding every twist and turn. It meant believing that God's plans, even if different from his own, were ultimately for his good.

In the grand adventure of faith, trusting God often feels like a wild roller coaster ride—thrilling, terrifying, and filled with those unexpected twists and turns. We all come to the table with our own unique set of challenges that can make trusting God feel like a high-stakes game of hide-and-seek. One moment, we're basking in the warmth of His promises, and the next, we're grappling with doubts that bubble up like an overzealous soda can. It's essential to recognize these challenges, not as roadblocks but as part of the colorful tapestry of our spiritual journeys.

One of the biggest challenges to trusting God is the frustration of unanswered prayers or unexpected outcomes. We naturally want to understand why certain things happen, but God's perspective is eternal, while ours is limited. Jeremiah 29:11 assures us that God's plans are always for our good, even when they differ from our own desires. Trusting God means believing that He sees the bigger picture and works all things for His purposes.

Psalm 13:1-2 captures the raw honesty of questioning God in times of uncertainty. David asks, "*How long, Lord? Will you forget me forever? How long will you hide your face from me?*" David's honesty shows us that it's okay to bring our doubts to God. Yet, by the end of the Psalm, David chooses trust, declaring, "*But I trust in your unfailing love*" (Psalm 13:5). This balance of honesty and trust is a powerful reminder that God welcomes our questions and calls us to trust Him through them.

Life's trials can shake our faith, but they are also opportunities to deepen our trust in God. Whether we face personal crises, financial struggles, or health issues, God uses these trials to strengthen our faith and draw us closer to Him. James 1:2-4 says, "*consider it pure joy, my brothers and sisters, whenever you face trials of many kinds, because you know that the testing of your faith produces perseverance.*"

Life has a knack for throwing curveballs just when you think everything is going according to plan. You might be cruising along, feeling secure in God's guidance, and then—bam!—you lose your job, a loved one falls ill, or you face a major life transition. Suddenly, the questions start flooding in. "Why would God let this happen?" "Where is He in all of this?" It's easy to feel like you're navigating a foggy road without a map. But here's the kicker: uncertainty can actually deepen our trust. It's a chance to lean into faith, even when the answers aren't readily available.

Another challenge is the weight of suffering. When the world around us feels heavy with pain, loss, and injustice, trusting God can seem like an uphill battle. It's perfectly normal to wrestle with the "why" of suffering, particularly when it feels senseless. But in those moments, we can find comfort in the stories of biblical figures who faced unimaginable hardships yet still clung to their faith.

Job's story (Job 1-42) is one of the Bible's most profound explorations of trust amid unanswered questions and trusting Him through trials and suffering. Job, while being a righteous man, endured unimaginable suffering and unimaginable loss, yet he continued to seek God, wrestling with his pain and confusion. And despite his suffering, he refused to curse God. He questioned, mourned, and struggled, but he ultimately trusted that God was still sovereign.

In Job 42:2, he finally declares, *"I know that You can do all things; no purpose of Yours can be thwarted."* Job's journey shows us that trust doesn't eliminate questions—it transforms them. In the end, Job's faith deepened, even though he never received all the answers. Eventually, God restored Job's fortunes, showing that trust in God, even in the darkest of times, leads to redemption.

Trials are not evidence of abandonment. In other words, difficulties in life don't mean that God has left us; they are often the way He refines our character. God is sovereign in our pain. Just as Job's suffering had a purpose, we can trust that God is in control, even when we can't see His plan. Perseverance builds trust. And enduring trials strengthens our trust in God, preparing us for greater things. God is a God of restoration—He doesn't leave us in our pain but ultimately brings healing and redemption. Ultimately, trusting God through trials allows us to hold on to hope, knowing that He works all things for our good.

Reflection Questions

- *What unanswered prayers or setbacks have challenged your trust in God?*

- *How can you rely on the testimony of God's past faithfulness to increase your trust in the future?*

- *How can you shift from seeking answers to seeking God's presence in times of uncertainty?*

Reflection Exercise

List one or two areas in your life where you feel frustrated by uncertainty or unanswered prayers. Write a prayer, expressing your feelings honestly to God. Ask Him to help you trust in His plan, even if you don't understand the reasons behind your current situation.

Building and Strengthening Trust through Thanksgiving

Building and strengthening trust is like nurturing a delicate garden; it requires attention, care, and the right environment to flourish. In our journey of faith, trust is the soil in which our relationships—both with God and others—are rooted. Just as a gardener must pull out weeds and ensure their plants receive ample sunlight, we too must actively cultivate trust in our lives. The good news? Trust can grow, and with the right biblical insights, we can create a thriving garden of faith that weathers life's storms.

A few of years ago, by recommendation of my wife, I decided to do a daily thankful journal. Each day, I'd write down something small I thanked God for. Some days, it was as simple as the fruit I had that day, while other days it was major things God had done for my family and me. This went on for a full year. Over time, I noticed a shift. These small, daily acts of thanksgiving began to change my heart, grounding me in the truth that God was faithful in both big and small things. And as I read my entries and looked back, my trust in Him increased.

You see, one night, as I looked back through the entries of my journal, some short and some long, I saw a pattern emerge. I could trace how God had been with me, answering prayers in ways I hadn't expected, but could now see clearly. I saw how blessed I was. And I realized that trust isn't something that just "happens"—it's built, one small step at a time, with thanksgiving and faith.

Building trust in God is an intentional process. Psalm 37:5 encourages us to *"commit your way to the Lord; trust in Him, and He will do this."* Trust isn't a passive feeling, but an active decision to place our lives in God's hands daily. Over time, as we entrust more to Him, we experience His faithfulness, which strengthens our trust.

Philippians 4:6-7 gives us a practical approach to building trust: *"Do not be anxious about anything, but in every situation, by prayer and petition, with thanksgiving, present your requests to God."* By bringing our worries to God, thanking Him for His faithfulness, and trusting Him with our concerns, we cultivate a trust that grows stronger with each prayer.

The Israelites' journey through the wilderness offers a vivid example of building trust in God day by day. In Exodus 16, God provided manna for the Israelites each morning, teaching them to rely on His provision. They couldn't store up manna for the future—they had to trust that God would provide what they needed, one day at a time. This daily dependence on God reminds us that trust is often built through consistent, small acts of faith, learning and choosing to rely on Him each day.

Isaiah 40:31 further encourages us, saying, *"But those who hope in the Lord will renew their strength. They will soar on wings like eagles; they will run and not grow weary, they will walk and not be faint."* Waiting on and thanking God strengthens our trust, allowing us to find renewed strength in His presence and promises.

Trusting God with Your Future Has Positive Outcomes

The future is filled with uncertainty, and it's easy to become anxious about what lies ahead. However, trusting God with our future means believing that He has a plan for our lives, a plan that is for our good. Jeremiah 29:11 says, *"For I know the plans I have for you,"* declares the Lord, *"plans to prosper you and not to harm you, plans to give you hope and a future."* And Matthew 6:34 adds, *"Therefore do not worry about tomorrow, for tomorrow will worry about itself. Each day has enough trouble of its own."*

The story of Joseph provides a powerful example of trusting God with the future. Joseph's story reminds us that God's plans for our future are always good, even when the path seems unclear. God has a plan for each of us, and we can trust that God's plans for our future are good and full of hope, even if we don't understand them right now. God's timing is also perfect, though it may not align with our own desires or expectations.

By trusting God with the future, we can release our anxieties and rest in His promises. Sometimes, trusting God with our future means waiting patiently for His direction, knowing that He will guide us at the right time. And just as God provided for Joseph, He will provide for us, opening doors and making a way when we trust in His plan.

Trusting God with the unknown future is a common source of anxiety and doubt for many believers. But we are called to trust God's plans, even when they diverge from our own expectations or desires. There are several Bible stories where characters put their trust in God even in the face of uncertainty, and this led to divine provision and guidance. These stories reinforce the message that God's ways are higher than ours. Trusting in God's promises fuels hope, reliance on His character fosters peace, and confidence in His plans drives purposeful living.

Living out one's faith means that trust in God is not just as a belief, but as a lifestyle. It involves daily decisions to rely on God, especially in moments when doubt seems easier. Trust in God influences our actions, decisions, and interactions with others, ultimately shaping our lives. Trust in God can also influence and transform communities. Personal faith acts as a catalyst for collective action, inspiring service, compassion, and positive change within communities. And putting your faith into action, such as volunteering, participating in community prayer groups, or supporting initiatives that align with biblical principles, makes a world of difference.

There is an intersection of faith and psychology. Belief in God affects mental and emotional well-being. Faith can lead to psychological resilience and a sense of purpose. In fact, there are many tangible benefits of transforming doubt into trust. For example, there are positive effects of faith on mental health, including reduced anxiety and depression, increased optimism, and a stronger sense of community.

So trust God with your future and embrace uncertainty by practicing daily surrender through prayer, focusing on the present moment, and finding peace in God's unchanging character. This will help you replace anxiety about the future with a confident trust in God's good and perfect plans.

Reflection Questions

- *What small steps can you take to build and strengthen your trust in God each day?*

- *How has God proven faithful to you in the past, and how does that encourage you to trust Him in the future?*

Reflection Exercise

Begin your own thankful/trusting journal. Start small: each day for a month, write down one thing that you are thankful for, and one thing that your are trusting God with, big or small. At the end of the month, look back and reflect on how this practice has impacted your faith. Ask God to help you build a foundation of trust that grows stronger with each step. If you are able, continue doing this journal for a full year. At the end of the year, read back all 365 entries, and you will see God has been so good to you.

Chapter 8

How Should I Live? The Call to Holiness

The Nature of Holiness

A S BELIEVERS IN CHRIST, we are called not just to believe, but to live in a way that reflects our faith. Holiness is more than moral perfection or a distant goal for super-saints; it is a practical and active pursuit for every Christian. It is about living a life that is set apart for God, dedicated to reflecting His character and values.

In the Old Testament, God called the nation of Israel to be a holy people (Leviticus 19), set apart from the other nations. God's instructions to Israel were not just about ceremonial cleanliness, but about living in a way that demonstrated His character to the world. Israel was called to be different, to reflect God's love, justice, and righteousness in their everyday lives. While they didn't always succeed, the call to holiness was central to their identity as God's people.

Holiness often feels like a lofty term reserved for saints and angels, a word that brings to mind images of glowing robes and heavenly choirs. At its core, however, holiness is about being set apart—not in a snooty, elitist way, but rather in a special, purpose-driven manner. Imagine it as a divine invitation to step into a life that reflects God's character. It's like being chosen as the lead singer in a heavenly choir; you're not just there to make noise—you're there to harmonize with God's will and purpose!

When I was a teenager, I noticed a phrase that seemed to come up often in church: "*Be holy, for I am holy.*" (Leviticus 19:2) I understood the importance of the message; but if I'm honest, I felt intimidated by it. Holiness seemed like a tall order—something that required perfection or saintly behavior. I found myself wondering, *Is holiness something I'm even capable of?*

As I dug deeper about the teaching of sanctification, I came across 1 Peter 1:15-16, which says, *"But just as He Who called you is holy, so be holy in all you do; for it is written: 'Be holy, because I am holy.'"* It became clear then that holiness wasn't just about perfection or moral behavior. I learned that holiness is not about being perfect. And thank God for that! Because if that were the case, we'd all be in trouble! Instead, I learned to think of holiness as a journey, a continuous path of growing closer to God while embracing the grace that covers our imperfections.

Essentially, we're all works in progress, and God isn't waiting for us to reach some unattainable spiritual plateau before He starts using us. In fact, it's often our flaws that make His grace shine even brighter. So since then, I've learned to understand holiness about being "set apart," about reflecting God's nature in our daily lives. Holiness is less about trying to reach a lofty standard and more about choosing to live in a way that aligns with God's heart and purposes.

Holiness is often misunderstood as a rigid set of rules or an unattainable standard. In reality, holiness means being set apart for God's purposes, living in a way that honors Him in every aspect of our lives. The holiness God calls us to is not merely about following rules, but about embracing His nature and allowing it to shape our character and behavior.

The Bible describes holiness as a reflection of God's character. To be holy is to be set apart for God, living in a way that honors Him. In Leviticus 20:26, God tells His people, *"You are to be holy to me because I, the Lord, am holy, and I have set you apart from the nations to be my own."* This verse highlights the essence of holiness: it's not about becoming "perfect" by human standards, but about dedicating ourselves to God and His purposes.

Romans 12:1-2 also encourages us to live a life of holiness, urging believers to *"offer your bodies as a living sacrifice, holy and pleasing to God—this is your true and proper worship."* Here, holiness is connected to worship. Living a holy life isn't something we do to earn God's love; instead, it is a response to His love. When we choose holiness, we align our lives with God's will, allowing Him to shape us into His image.

The prophet Isaiah's vision of God in Isaiah 6 offers a powerful insight into holiness. Isaiah sees the Lord seated on a throne, with angels calling, *"Holy, holy, holy is the Lord*

Almighty." Overwhelmed by God's holiness, Isaiah is deeply aware of his own sinfulness. Yet, God purifies him, demonstrating that holiness is a transformative process. Isaiah's vision reminds us that encountering God's holiness doesn't leave us unchanged—it draws us closer to Him, transforming our lives.

This transformation is echoed in 2 Corinthians 7:1, where Paul encourages believers to "*purify ourselves from everything that contaminates body and spirit, perfecting holiness out of reverence for God.*" Holiness, then, is a journey, a commitment to letting God shape us to reflect His love, purity, and goodness.

Holiness is also deeply relational. It's not just about following rules or checking off boxes on a spiritual to-do list. It's about cultivating a relationship with God and allowing that relationship to transform who you are. Think of it like a friendship—when you spend time with someone you admire, their qualities tend to rub off on you. The more we engage with God through prayer, Scripture, and community, the more His holiness seeps into our lives. We begin to reflect His love, patience, and kindness—not because we're trying really hard, but because we're becoming more like Him through our connection.

Another fascinating aspect of holiness is its communal nature. It's not just an individual pursuit; it's meant to be shared! Picture a vibrant garden where each flower is unique, yet part of a beautiful tapestry. When we live out our holiness together, we create a supportive environment that encourages others to grow in their faith. This means being vulnerable with one another, sharing our struggles and victories, and reminding each other of our shared identity in Christ. After all, if holiness is about reflecting God's character, what better way to do that than in fellowship with our brothers and sisters in faith?

And holiness is also about mission. We're called to be light in a world that can sometimes feel overwhelmingly dark. When we embrace our holiness, we become agents of change, reflecting God's love and grace to those around us. It's like being a beacon on a hill—impossible to miss! Whether it's through acts of kindness, standing up for justice, or simply showing compassion, our holy lives can inspire others to seek out the divine as well. So, let's embrace the nature of holiness not just as a lofty ideal, but as an exciting adventure that invites us into a deeper relationship with God and a transformative impact on the world around us.

Living a Life Set Apart

Holiness means being set apart for God. It means to be dedicated to God, living a life that reflects His nature and purposes. Our call to holiness is rooted in the character of God. We are holy because He is holy, and He empowers us to live in His holiness. Holiness isn't confined to weekend worship or spiritual moments; it's about how we live daily in our relationships, work, and personal choices.

Holiness is transformational, because as we pursue holiness, God's Spirit works within us to transform our hearts, minds, and actions to reflect His will. Holiness is NOT legalism. Pursuing holiness is not about rigid rule-keeping, but a dynamic relationship with God that shapes how we live and love. And to live a holy life is to live differently from the world around us. While the world promotes self-centeredness, materialism, and moral compromise, God calls us to live in a way that is distinct. In 1 Thessalonians 4:7, Paul reminds us, *"For God did not call us to be impure, but to live a holy life."*

The story of Daniel provides a powerful example of living a holy life in a corrupt culture (Daniel 1, 6). Despite living in Babylon, a society that did not honor God, Daniel remained committed to living a holy life. He refused to defile himself with the king's food and later risked his life by continuing to pray to God despite a royal decree forbidding it. Daniel's life of holiness stood out, and God used him to bring honor to His name in a foreign land.

Daniel's story teaches us that holiness requires distinction. To live a holy life means living differently from the world—our values, priorities, and actions should reflect God's kingdom, not worldly standards. It is a daily choice. And like Daniel, we must make daily choices that align with God's will, even when those choices go against the grain of culture or personal convenience.

Holiness honors God and impacts others because when we live holy lives, others notice, and it becomes an opportunity to reflect God's glory and point them to Christ. That is why living a life set apart for God often requires courage to stand firm in faith, especially when the world pressures us to conform. But we are not called to live holy lives by our own strength; the Holy Spirit equips and empowers us to live in a way that honors God.

At the heart of holiness is love—love for God and love for others. Holiness is not just about personal purity, but about how we reflect God's love in our relationships and communities. A truly holy life is marked by compassion, justice, and service to others. Love is the ultimate expression of holiness. This is why Jesus commanded in Matthew 22:37-39, *"'Love the Lord your God with all your heart and with all your soul and with all your mind.' This is the first and greatest commandment. And the second is like it: 'Love your neighbor as yourself.'"*

The Good Samaritan (Luke 10:25-37) is a profound illustration of how holiness is expressed through love. In this parable, Jesus challenges the religious leaders of His time by showing that true holiness is not about rigid religious practices but about showing mercy and love to those in need. The Samaritan, considered an outsider by the Jews, demonstrated what it meant to live a life of love and compassion, which Jesus holds up as the example of what it means to be a neighbor and live out our faith.

Holiness is best expressed through love, and a life of holiness is marked by genuine love for God and others. If we claim holiness but lack love, we have missed the heart of what it means to be holy. Holiness calls us to care for the vulnerable with compassion and empathy, fight for justice, and show mercy to those in need, just as Jesus did. Like the Samaritan, holy love crosses cultural, social, and racial boundaries to serve others in Christ's name.

True holiness is not lived in isolation, but in community, as we show God's love to those around us. It is relational. And the more we grow in holiness, the more our hearts will reflect God's heart for people, leading us to serve, care for, and love others deeply.

Reflection Questions

- *How does the idea of being "set apart" for God change your perspective on holiness?*

- *What are areas in your life where God may be calling you to pursue greater holiness?*

- *What choices can you make today that align with living a holy life, even if they go against the world's values?*

- *How does your love for others reflect your pursuit of holiness? In what ways can you grow in showing love and compassion?*

Reflection Exercise

Write down one or more areas of your life where you sense a need to be "set apart" for God, such as your relationships, work, or personal habits. Reflect on practical steps you can take to honor God in this area(s). Pray for His guidance and strength as you commit to this journey of holiness.

Living Out Holiness

For many people, the idea of holiness might seem daunting, almost like trying to climb a mountain while juggling flaming torches. But holiness is less about rigid rules and more about a delightful dance with God, where every step is infused with grace. Imagine taking a stroll with a friend—sometimes you skip, sometimes you twirl, but the joy of being together is what matters most.

As we strut down this path of holiness, we'll encounter challenges that may trip us up. Maybe it's the coworker who knows just how to push your buttons or the endless notifications pulling you away from prayer time. But here's where the fun begins: overcoming these hurdles can turn into opportunities for growth! Picture yourself as a superhero, equipped with the powerful tools of prayer and Scripture. Every time you respond to negativity with grace or choose to help someone in need, you're flexing your holiness muscles, growing stronger in faith and character.

After a major career change, I learned to live out holiness in a practical way during my daily interactions. Allow me to explain. My two previous jobs were at Christian environments, first as a youth and young adult pastor, and then as a dean at a Christian university. For a decade-and-a-half, my job required of me to be an example. However, unfortunately, that wasn't always the case. And I would also love to say that these environments and my example were always pure, but I would lie if I did. Nonetheless, being surrounded by believers was certainly great. The job environments, though not perfect, were conducive to good living.

But fast forward a few years, and after changing careers and working in the public sector, I noticed things were not the same. When I started working at a new job at a public school, I quickly noticed that the office culture was filled with gossip and negativity. At times, I found it difficult to avoid getting sucked into conversations that felt toxic. This didn't feel right.

After praying for wisdom, I felt God prompting me to take a stand, to be a light in that environment rather than just blending in. With intentionality, I began to redirect conversations toward positive topics and chose to refrain from speaking negatively about others. I am not saying I was (or that I am) perfect; far from it. However, over time, my coworkers noticed the difference, and some even began to follow this example. This choice to live out holiness became a testimony to those around, showing that holiness isn't about separating ourselves from the world, but about bringing God's love and goodness into the world.

I've now learned that living out holiness means allowing our lives to reflect God's character in everything we do. Hebrews 12:14 encourages us to *"make every effort to live in peace with everyone and to be holy; without holiness, no one will see the Lord."* This verse reminds us that our holiness is a witness to others, allowing them to see God through our actions.

Colossians 3:12-14 gives us a practical description of holy living: *"Therefore, as God's chosen people, holy and dearly loved, clothe yourselves with compassion, kindness, humility, gentleness, and patience... And over all these virtues put on love, which binds them all together in perfect unity."* Holiness is not just about avoiding certain behaviors; it's about embracing qualities that reflect God's love and mercy.

The life of Daniel offers a powerful example of living out holiness. Despite being in a foreign land with different customs, Daniel remained faithful to God's standards. In Daniel 1, he refused to eat the king's food, choosing instead to honor God's clearly established dietary laws. Later, in Daniel 6, he continued to pray openly despite a law that prohibited worship of anyone other than the king. Daniel's choices to honor God, even when it set him apart, made him a witness of God's power and faithfulness.

Holiness doesn't require isolation from the world; it requires courage and consistency in reflecting God's values, even in environments that challenge our faith. By choosing holiness, we become lights in a dark world, pointing others toward God's goodness. Holiness is not an unattainable standard, but a daily journey of growing in Christlikeness, empowered by God's Spirit. As we pursue holiness, we reflect God's nature to the world, bringing glory to Him in all that we do.

The concept of holiness often conjures images of solemn faces, cloistered monks, and an abundance of rules. But holiness is not just about restriction; it's an invitation to a divine party of joy, purpose, and connection with God. Being holy isn't about perfection either; it's about progression. It's a delightful journey with God as our guide, leading us to navigate life's challenges with grace.

And holiness is contagious. When you choose to live a life set apart for God, you become a beacon of hope and inspiration to those around you. Picture this: you walk into a room filled with negativity, and your holy vibes instantly uplift the atmosphere. Your friends and family might start to notice that you approach life with a different outlook, a zest for living that's infectious. They may even ask you, "What's your secret?" And that's your chance to share the joy of holiness, inviting them to join the dance of divine living. It's an opportunity to spread light in a world that often feels dim.

Reflection Questions

- *What are some practical ways you can live out holiness in your daily interactions?*

- *How does choosing holiness impact your relationships and influence others?*

- *How can you allow the Holy Spirit to empower you to live a life of holiness in practical ways this week?*

Reflection Exercise

Identify one specific behavior or attitude you'd like to change to reflect God's holiness more closely in your life. Write down an action plan, outlining small steps you can take each day to align this area with God's values. Pray for strength and consistency as you work on living out holiness.

The Power of Holiness

When my family and I moved to the United States, I was a teenager. It was a very difficult time in my life. Thankfully, we quickly found a church-community that was the best thing that could've happened to us. I'll never forget the love we found in this community. I quickly learned that this church was known for its kindness and generosity. The people there had a unique warmth, and their love for God was evident in every aspect of their lives. They were known not just for their words, but for their actions, helping one another in practical ways, welcoming strangers, and going out of their way to serve those in need. They reminded me of Jesus' words in Matthew 5:16: "*Let your light shine before others, that they may see your good deeds and glorify your Father in heaven.*"

This community had a powerful impact on everyone who came in contact with them. People would leave changed, inspired to know God more deeply. This community showed me that holiness, when lived out collectively, has the power to transform lives and bring people closer to God.

Holiness isn't just a personal pursuit; it has a ripple effect on those around us. When we choose to live holy lives, we become witnesses of God's love, drawing others toward Him. In 1 Thessalonians 4:7, Paul reminds believers, *"For God did not call us to be impure, but to live a holy life."* Holiness is part of our calling as Christians, empowering us to reflect God's character and advance His kingdom.

Holiness also prepares us for God's work. In 2 Timothy 2:21, Paul writes, *"Those who cleanse themselves from the latter will be instruments for special purposes, made holy, useful to the Master, and prepared to do any good work."* When we pursue holiness, we become more aligned with God's will, ready to be used by Him to impact others.

The Early Church in Acts 2:42-47 exemplifies the power of collective holiness. This community was known for its unity, generosity, and dedication to prayer and worship. Their lives reflected God's love so vividly that *"the Lord added to their number daily those who were being saved."* The Early Church's commitment to holiness created an environment where God's presence was tangible, drawing people to faith and transforming their community.

Holiness, then, is not just about personal growth; it's a tool God uses to reach others. When we live holy lives, we become *"salt and light"* (Matthew 5:13-14), enhancing the lives of those around us and pointing them toward a relationship with God.

Reflection Questions

- *How can your pursuit of holiness impact your family, friends, or community?*

- *What steps can you take to create an environment of holiness in your relationships or community?*

Reflection Exercise

Think about your sphere of influence—your family, friends, school, workplace, or church. Write down two or three ways you can contribute to a culture of holiness within these groups. Pray, asking God to help you be a light and a source of encouragement to those around you, that they may see His love through your actions.

Chapter 9

What Is the Role of Community in My Faith?

The Biblical Model of Community

F AITH IS OFTEN VIEWED as a deeply personal journey between the believer and God. While this is true, the Bible consistently highlights the importance of community in our spiritual growth and perseverance. The Christian faith is not meant to be lived in isolation but in fellowship with other believers. Community plays a critical role in the development of our faith, and it is twofold First, we contribute to the spiritual well-being of others, and we also find strength, encouragement, and accountability through Christian fellowship.

When I was a freshman at college, my brother, our roommates, and a few other friends started a ministry group. While small at first, this ministry eventually grew to over one-hundred students. This group became my family and my safe space. Over time, something incredible happened. That group became a church where we could share our struggles and joys without fear of judgment. We found encouragement, accountability, and support in ways I hadn't imagined. I remember one evening in particular when I shared a personal challenge, and the group rallied around me in prayer, offering words of comfort and wisdom. That night, I felt the power of community like never before.

It reminded me of Hebrews 10:24-25, which encourages us to *"consider how we may spur one another on toward love and good deeds, not giving up meeting together... but encouraging one another."* Community, I learned, isn't just a social gathering; it's a place where we help each other grow and walk more closely with God.

The Bible places great importance on living in community. God designed us for relationships, and through Christian community, we find encouragement, support, and accountability. Hebrews 10:24-25 emphasizes the role of community in spurring one another on in faith and good works. This "spurring" isn't about criticism or pressure; it's about mutual encouragement, helping each other live out our faith with love and purpose.

Acts 2:42-47 gives us a beautiful picture of the Early Church, a community devoted to *"the apostles' teaching and to fellowship, to the breaking of bread and to prayer."* This was the perfect example of the biblical foundation for community. This early Christian community shared their lives deeply, meeting each other's needs and growing in faith together. Through this example, we see that Christian community is about more than just gathering—it's about creating a space where we support and grow with one another.

After the Holy Spirit descended at Pentecost, believers devoted themselves to the apostles' teaching, to fellowship, to breaking bread together, and to prayer. They shared their possessions and supported one another, reflecting a deep sense of unity and belonging. This vibrant community drew others to the faith and resulted in many being saved daily.

But it's not just in the Early Church that we find this example; the concept of community is woven into the fabric of Scripture, beginning with God's creation of humanity. Community is foundational to the Christian faith, rooted in both the Old and New Testaments. From the early Israelites to the church in the New Testament, God's people were never meant to walk alone.

From the very beginning, in Genesis 2:18 we read. *"The Lord God said, 'It is not good for the man to be alone. I will make a helper suitable for him.'"* Then, the wise man said in Ecclesiastes 4:9-10, *"Two are better than one, because they have a good return for their labor: If either of them falls down, one can help the other up."* And in Hebrews 10:24-25 we read, *"And let us consider how we may spur one another on toward love and good deeds, not giving up meeting together, as some are in the habit of doing, but encouraging one another—and all the more as you see the Day approaching."* Galatians 6:2 calls believers to *"carry each other's burdens, and in this way, you will fulfill the law of Christ."*

These verses speak to the heart of community: we are called to help bear each other's burdens, offering support, compassion, and encouragement. Just as Christ carried our burdens on the cross, we are to reflect His love by walking alongside others in their struggles and joys.

The Early Church's commitment to fellowship, prayer, and shared resources in Acts 2 shows that community involves a selfless investment in each other's lives. This model demonstrates how believers can fulfill the "law of Christ"—to love one another—in tangible, practical ways.

The Benefits of Christian Fellowship

Community strengthens faith. Just as in the Early Church, a strong Christian community can encourage spiritual growth and perseverance through challenges and mutual support. Being part of a community offers accountability in our spiritual walk. We are encouraged to *"spur one another on toward love and good deeds."* Jesus promised that when two or more gather in His name, He is there with them (Matthew 18:20), emphasizing the significance of communal worship and fellowship.

Christian fellowship is more than just gathering together. It provides believers with a sense of belonging, support, and encouragement. In times of trial, the love and care from fellow believers can help sustain us. Community fosters spiritual health and growth. 1 Thessalonians 5:11 says, *"Therefore encourage one another and build each other up, just as in fact you are doing."*

Paul's relationship with the church at Philippi illustrates the deep connection that can exist within Christian communities. Even while imprisoned, Paul found joy and encouragement from the Philippians' prayers and support. Their fellowship with him in the gospel fostered a sense of unity that transcended physical distance, demonstrating how spiritual bonds can strengthen and uplift believers.

As believers, we are members of one body (Romans 12; 1 Corinthians 12), each playing a unique role in the church. Fellowship provides emotional and spiritual support, especially during trials. Sharing experiences, learning from each other's faith journeys, and praying together help us grow spiritually. A strong community is characterized by acts of service and generosity, just as the Early Church members shared their possessions. Communities that are united in their mission to spread the gospel provide strength and clarity in living out God's purpose.

Reflection Questions

- *How has community impacted your spiritual journey so far?*

- *What can you do to build deeper connections within your faith community?*

- *In what ways can you contribute to fostering a stronger sense of fellowship in your church or small group?*

- *How can you show love and support to someone in your faith community this week?*

Reflection Exercise

Think of a way you can support someone in your community this week, whether through prayer, encouragement, or a small act of service. Write down how you plan to reach out, and pray for God's guidance in creating a space where others feel supported and loved.

Challenges and Blessings of Community

Two of my closest friends had a falling out years ago. Misunderstandings and differing opinions had built up over time, creating tension between them. At first, they both avoided dealing with it, hoping the issues would resolve on their own. But the distance grew, and this affected the larger group of friends. Thankfully, they eventually had a difficult, but honest conversation. Through tears and apologies, they forgave each other, and their friendship became stronger than ever.

That experience taught me that community isn't always easy, but the effort is worth it. Colossians 3:13 encourages us to *"bear with each other and forgive one another if any of you has a grievance against someone."* Forgiving each other can be challenging, but it's also deeply healing. When we choose to let go of bitterness, we make room for God's grace to work in our relationships.

Community comes with its challenges. Differences in personality, opinions, and backgrounds can create tension. However, the blessings of community far outweigh the difficulties. In fact, there is power in diversity! Colossians 3:13 reminds us that we are called to *"bear with each other"* and extend forgiveness. This means practicing patience, compassion, and a willingness to work through conflicts.

Ephesians 4:2-3 echoes this, saying, *"Be completely humble and gentle; be patient, bearing with one another in love. Make every effort to keep the unity of the Spirit through the bond of peace."* Community isn't about perfection; it's about showing grace and humility as we navigate our relationships. This creates an environment where we can grow spiritually and become a stronger witness to the world.

Creating and maintaining a strong Christian community requires intentional effort. Colossians 3:12-14 says, *"Therefore, as God's chosen people, holy and dearly loved, clothe yourselves with compassion, kindness, humility, gentleness and patience. Bear with each other and forgive one another... And over all these virtues put on love, which binds them all together in perfect unity."*

When Saul, later known as Paul, first converted to Christianity, the other disciples were wary of him due to his past persecution of believers. However, Barnabas stepped in, vouching for Saul and welcoming him into the community. Barnabas' encouragement and support helped Saul integrate into the Early Church, showing the transformative power of acceptance and love in a community.

Paul and Barnabas had a sharp disagreement in Acts 15:36-41, leading them to part ways in ministry. Yet, both continued to serve faithfully, demonstrating that disagreements don't have to destroy unity or hinder God's work. Their story reminds us that conflict is a natural part of relationships, but doesn't have to mean the end of connection or respect.

1 Corinthians 12:12 emphasizes that believers are part of one body with many parts. Each member has a unique role, and our differences should be viewed as strengths rather than obstacles. This perspective encourages us to value diversity within community and to handle challenges with grace, recognizing that each person contributes something important to the body of Christ.

Building community starts with humility, patience, and a willingness to bear with one another in love. Conflicts are inevitable, but communities that practice forgiveness and love can overcome challenges and grow stronger. Christian communities should be places of refuge for all, where everyone feels valued and accepted. Acts of service, both within the community and to the outside world, help maintain a sense of purpose and mission.

Reflection Questions

- *What are some challenges you face in your community, and how can you respond with grace and humility?*

- *How can you see disagreements or differences as opportunities for growth and deeper understanding?*

- *Reflect on a time when your Christian community helped you through a difficult season. How did that experience shape your faith?*

Reflection Exercise

Think of a relationship or situation in your life that has caused tension. Write a prayer, asking God to help you approach this situation with patience, humility, and a desire for unity. Consider reaching out to the person involved, if appropriate, with a spirit of forgiveness or understanding.

Building a Strong Christian Community

When I was in college, a group of us from my ministry decided to start a community outreach project. We would gather regularly to brainstorm ways to serve our local area, from hosting free meals to organizing school supply drives. What amazed me most was the way this shared mission deepened our relationships. We weren't just meeting for ourselves; we were meeting to make a difference. The interesting thing about this all, ironically, was that most of us had no means and would ourselves had benefited from support from others. However, this helped us look beyond our personal needs and selflessly think on how to help others.

Our group became close, praying for each other's needs, supporting each other's dreams, and celebrating each other's victories. Matthew 18:20 reminds us that *"where two or three gather in My name, there am I with them."* In serving together, we experienced God's presence in powerful ways, and our bonds grew stronger because we were united by a shared purpose.

Building a strong Christian community takes intentionality. Romans 12:10 encourages us to *"be devoted to one another in love. Honor one another above yourselves."* Community thrives when each member shows love, respect, and a willingness to serve. When we prioritize the well-being of others and look for ways to support each other, we create an environment where everyone feels valued.

1 Thessalonians 5:11 adds, *"Therefore encourage one another and build each other up, just as in fact you are doing."* Encouragement is essential for a healthy community. By

speaking life into each other's faith journeys, we strengthen our bonds and become more resilient together.

Jesus' selection of His disciples demonstrates a powerful model of community. He brought together individuals with different personalities, backgrounds, and even political views, yet they united around a shared mission. Despite their differences, they learned from each other, grew together, and built a foundation for the Early Church.

This unity didn't come from avoiding differences but from embracing them, with Christ at the center. Following Jesus' example, we can build communities that reflect God's love and truth, prioritizing unity and purpose over personal preferences.

Reflection Questions

- *How can you actively contribute to building a strong, supportive Christian community?*

- *What steps can you take to encourage and uplift others in your church or small group?*

Reflection Exercise

Write down one or two ways you can be a source of encouragement or support within your community. This might be through offering prayer, serving in a ministry, or reaching out to someone in need. Ask God to use you as a light within your community, helping to create a space where others feel supported and encouraged in their faith.

Chapter 10

How Do I Persevere in Faith?

The Need for Perseverance

PERSEVERANCE IS LIKE THAT stubborn little weed that grows in your garden, refusing to give up even when you've tried to pull it out. It is resilience in action. In our spiritual journey, we often encounter challenges that feel insurmountable, but it's in these moments that our faith is truly tested. Just as the Apostle Paul reminds us in Romans 5:3-5, suffering brings perseverance, and perseverance brings hope. So, if you ever feel like giving up because life has thrown yet another curveball your way, remember that every trial is a divine invitation to grow and deepen your faith.

Recently, my wife went through one of the toughest seasons of her life. Nothing seemed to go right at work, and every day felt like a battle. She would come home every day crying, which would break my heart. Our kids would notice, and it affected them as well. She would work so hard, only for people to criticize and spread lies. Numerous times, we found ourselves asking, *Is this worth it? Can we really keep going?* In those difficult moments, I was reminded of a verse that had given me strength before: *"Blessed is the one who perseveres under trial because, having stood the test, that person will receive the crown of life that the Lord has promised to those who love Him"* (James 1:12).

Reading those words again gave me a new perspective. I realized that God wasn't asking us to have all the answers or feel strong every day; He was asking us to stay faithful. That verse reminded me that perseverance wasn't about perfection, but about holding on to

God through every struggle. It didn't make my wife's challenges disappear, but it gave us hope that God was with her and that there was a purpose to her endurance.

Perseverance is essential to the Christian journey. James 1:12 highlights the blessing of enduring trials, promising the *"crown of life"* to those who persevere. This "crown" isn't simply a reward for making it through difficult times; it represents the deepening of our faith, our character, and our relationship with God.

Faith is not just a one-time decision, but an ongoing journey. The Bible calls us to a faith that endures, especially through trials, hardships, and uncertainties. Perseverance is key to maintaining our faith in God and living out His purpose for us. Hebrews 12:1-2 encourages us to *"run with perseverance the race marked out for us, fixing our eyes on Jesus."* The Christian life is often described as a race, and perseverance is what keeps us moving forward, even when we feel like giving up. By focusing on Jesus, Who endured the cross for our sake, we find strength to keep running, knowing that our faith journey is leading us closer to Him.

Job's story in the Old Testament is one of the Bible's clearest examples of perseverance. Despite losing everything—his family, health, and possessions—Job held onto his faith. While he wrestled with deep questions and even doubted at times, he ultimately trusted in God's sovereignty and goodness. Job didn't throw in the towel. Instead, he clung to his faith, demonstrating that perseverance is not merely about enduring hardship but about maintaining hope in the face of despair. And in the end, God restored Job's fortunes, honoring his perseverance. Job's story shows us that faith can endure even the darkest trials and that God is faithful to those who trust in Him.

And don't forget about Moses. Talk about a man who had to persevere! From his early days in a basket on the Nile to the daunting task of leading the Israelites out of Egypt, Moses faced numerous challenges, including some really cranky people. Yet, he continued to press on, trusting in God's plan. His perseverance wasn't just for his benefit; it paved the way for an entire nation to experience freedom. So, when you find yourself in a tough spot, think of Moses and remember that your perseverance might just be the key to unlocking someone else's miracle.

Romans 5:3-4 further illustrates this, teaching that *"suffering produces perseverance; perseverance, character; and character, hope."* Through our struggles, God is shaping us, building resilience in our hearts, and strengthening our hope in Him. As much as I would like to say that all things ended up working out for my wife, the truth is that there are still struggles. And yet, thankfully, with God's grace, she is much happier and at peace, and much more resilient than ever before.

The Biblical Call to Persevere

Perseverance in faith is a central theme throughout Scripture. It is not merely about survival, but about growth and steadfastness in the face of trials. The Bible encourages believers to endure and remain faithful, especially when faced with difficulties. James 1:12 states, *"Blessed is the one who perseveres under trial because, having stood the test, that person will receive the crown of life that the Lord has promised to those who love him."* And Romans 5:3-4 adds, *"Not only so, but we also glory in our sufferings, because we know that suffering produces perseverance; perseverance, character; and character, hope."*

Job's story is one of ultimate perseverance. Even when he did not understand why he was suffering, Job continued to believe that God was sovereign. In the end, Job's perseverance was rewarded as God restored everything he had lost and more. Job's faith through suffering exemplifies how perseverance in the hardest moments brings about spiritual growth and divine reward.

Trials are not pointless; they are refining moments that build godly character and deepen our trust in God. Perseverance builds character. The Bible teaches that enduring hardship is often part of God's plan to strengthen and shape us. And although they can seem overwhelming, the trials we face are temporary compared to the eternal rewards of remaining faithful. God has promised eternal rewards for those who persevere, including the "crown of life" for those who endure. But perseverance requires trusting God even when our feelings or circumstances might lead us to doubt.

Persevering in faith requires more than just knowledge of Scripture; it involves practical, daily steps that help us stay connected to God and rooted in His promises. Philippians 4:6-7 says, *"Do not be anxious about anything, but in every situation, by prayer and petition, with thanksgiving, present your requests to God. And the peace of God, which transcends all understanding, will guard your hearts and your minds in Christ Jesus."*

Thankfully, Jesus' words in Matthew 11:28-30 are a powerful reminder that we do not have to carry the burdens of life alone. He invites all who are weary and burdened to come to Him for rest. This invitation is not only for physical rest but for spiritual renewal and strength. Jesus' promise of rest is essential for persevering in faith, as it reminds us that we can rely on Him for the strength to continue, even when we feel like giving up.

Perseverance in faith requires constant communication with God. Prayer is our lifeline to divine strength and guidance. We cannot persevere in our own strength. It is only through reliance on God's power that we are able to endure. That is why Jesus invites us to find rest in Him. This rest is essential for renewing our strength and continuing in faith. Perseverance is a daily decision to trust God and follow His lead, no matter what obstacles come our way.

Divine guidance is the key to navigating life's valleys with faith and hope. It is the map for persevering through any difficulty. There is a critical importance in listening to God's voice during our lowest points. God speaks to us in different ways: through Scripture, prayer, the Holy Spirit, and the counsel of others. Each of these communications can offer guidance, comfort, and reassurance during trials. I encourage you to cultivate a listening heart, open to discerning God's message amidst the noise of struggles, trials, and pain.

Reflection Questions

- *When have you experienced a season that tested your faith? How did God help you persevere?*

- *What does it mean to you that perseverance is part of God's process of refining your character and building hope?*

- *In what ways can you strengthen your connection to God and your community to help you persevere in faith?*

Reflection Exercise

Write down a recent challenge that has tested your perseverance. Reflect on how God has been present with you in that situation, even if it's still unresolved. Then, pray, asking God to strengthen your faith and give you the resilience to keep trusting Him, no matter what lies ahead.

Faith Amid Suffering

I still remember a conversation I had with my wife while she was going through this extremely difficult time mentioned above. As a result of all the stress and challenges, she was facing the loss of friendships, health struggles, and a series of setbacks that made her question her faith. One day, with tears, she told me, "I feel like I'm clinging on to God with just my fingertips, but I'm still holding on." Her honesty moved me, and it reminded me of Jesus' words in John 16:33: *"In this world, you will have trouble. But take heart! I have overcome the world."*

Her perseverance taught me that faith isn't always about feeling strong; sometimes, it's simply about not letting go. When we face suffering, faith becomes a daily decision—a choice to hold on to God, even when we don't understand why we're suffering. And through this choice, God is there, offering comfort and strength that may not change our circumstances, but transforms our hearts.

Suffering is an inevitable part of life, and the Bible doesn't shy away from this reality. Jesus warned His followers that they would face hardship, but He also promised His presence and victory over all circumstances. John 16:33 reminds us that, even in suffering, we have reason to hope because Jesus has already overcome.

Romans 8:18 brings an eternal perspective, saying, *"I consider that our present sufferings are not worth comparing with the glory that will be revealed in us."* This verse doesn't diminish our pain, but it gives it context, reminding us that there is a future glory awaiting us that will surpass any suffering we endure now. Our faith, tested by suffering, prepares us for this eternal glory, deepening our reliance on God and our understanding of His love.

Paul's perseverance amid suffering is one of the New Testament's most inspiring examples of faith. Throughout his ministry, Paul endured imprisonment, beatings, and even shipwrecks. In 2 Corinthians 12:9-10, Paul shares that despite asking God to remove a *"thorn in the flesh,"* God responded, *"My grace is sufficient for you, for My power is made perfect in weakness."* Paul's response? *"I delight in weaknesses... For when I am weak, then I am strong."*

Paul's story shows us that God's strength often shines brightest in our weakest moments. Rather than removing all our challenges, God offers His grace and presence, empowering us to endure and grow stronger in our faith.

A key to perseverance in faith is maintaining an eternal perspective. When we focus on the bigger picture of God's plan and His promises for eternity, we are better equipped to face the temporary challenges of life. Paul reminds us in 2 Corinthians 4:17-18, *"For our light and momentary troubles are achieving for us an eternal glory that far outweighs them all. So we fix our eyes not on what is seen, but on what is unseen, since what is seen is temporary, but what is unseen is eternal.*" He then adds in Colossians 3:2, "*Set your minds on things above, not on earthly things.*"

Paul endured incredible hardships for the sake of the gospel—imprisonment, beatings, shipwrecks, and threats on his life. Yet, he never wavered in his faith. Paul was able to persevere because he kept his focus on the eternal reward, not on his immediate sufferings. He wrote in 2 Corinthians that his "*light and momentary troubles*" were achieving for him an eternal glory that far outweighed them all. Paul's perseverance was rooted in his eternal perspective, making him a powerful example for us.

Trials can seem overwhelming when we focus only on the present. Keeping an eternal perspective helps us see beyond the immediate. The Bible promises that our perseverance will be rewarded in eternity, motivating us to remain steadfast. Though suffering is painful, it is not permanent. God's eternal kingdom offers an everlasting reward. When we fix our minds on eternity, we find hope and strength to endure the present. Even when we don't understand why we are facing certain trials, we can trust that God's ultimate plan is good.

Reflection Questions

- *Reflect on a time when you experienced God's strength carrying you through a difficult season. How did that experience impact your faith?*

- *How does knowing that Jesus has "overcome the world" give you hope during suffering?*

- *When have you experienced God's strength in moments of weakness?*

Reflection Exercise

Write a short prayer expressing any pain or challenges you're currently facing. Acknowledge the difficulties honestly, then ask God to help you experience His strength in your weakness. Close by thanking Him for His presence and the promise of future glory beyond this suffering.

Strengthening Perseverance

When I was younger, a mentor once gave me a piece of advice that has stayed with me through difficult seasons. He told me, "Perseverance isn't something you wait for—it's something you build, one day at a time." He explained how small, daily acts of faith, like prayer, reading Scripture, and spending time with God, build a foundation of resilience. "When the storms come," he said, "you'll find that you're stronger than you realized because you've been rooted in God."

Taking his advice, I began to see my daily walk with God as preparation. Each prayer, each moment of surrender, was like adding strength to my foundation. When challenges arose, I found that my perseverance had grown, not by accident, but by the daily choice to build my faith.

Strengthening perseverance is a process, built through regular practices that deepen our relationship with God. Psalm 37:5 encourages us to *"commit your way to the Lord; trust in Him, and He will do this."* Perseverance isn't just about surviving trials—it's about building a faith that endures by staying close to God.

Philippians 4:6-7 gives us a practical approach to cultivating perseverance, saying, *"Do not be anxious about anything, but in every situation, by prayer and petition, with thanksgiving, present your requests to God."* By bringing our worries to God in prayer, we exchange anxiety for peace and build a resilience that can face life's challenges. Thanksgiving, even in hardship, reinforces our faith, reminding us of God's faithfulness.

The Israelites' journey through the wilderness is a powerful example of building perseverance. Each day, they relied on God to provide manna, learning to trust His provision daily. Exodus 16 teaches us that perseverance isn't about storing up strength for tomorrow; it's about daily dependence on God. Jesus echoed this in Matthew 6:34, saying, *"Do not worry about tomorrow, for tomorrow will worry about itself."*

By focusing on each day, trusting God for today's needs, we gradually build a foundation of perseverance. Our strength grows as we experience God's faithfulness one day at a time, equipping us to face future challenges with greater faith and resilience.

Staying in the Race and Finishing The Race

Staying in the race is more than just a catchy phrase; it's a vibrant call to action for every Christian navigating the often-bumpy roads of life. Imagine that you're in a marathon, surrounded by cheering crowds and well-meaning friends, yet your legs feel like lead and your spirit is starting to wane. Sound familiar? Life can sometimes feel like that marathon, where the finish line seems miles away and the temptation to throw in the towel is ever-present. Thankfully, the Bible offers us divine insights that can keep us moving forward, no matter how heavy the burden may feel.

First, let's talk about endurance—an essential ingredient in our spiritual toolkit. Hebrews 12:1 encourages us to *"run with perseverance the race marked out for us."* This isn't just a suggestion; it's a divine command. Think of endurance as your secret weapon. Imagine a runner who trains tirelessly, building strength and resilience. Similarly, our faith muscles need regular workouts. Prayer, worship, and diving into Scripture help us to build our spiritual endurance. The more we invest in our relationship with God, the less likely we are to stumble when life throws those curveballs our way.

Now, let's not forget that every great race has its supporters! Surrounding ourselves with a community of fellow believers can be a game-changer. Just as the crowd cheers on the runners, our friends and family can uplift us when the going gets tough. Ecclesiastes 4:9-10 reminds us that *"two are better than one."* When we stumble, a friend can help us back up, and when we feel weary, their encouragement can breathe new life into our spirits. So, don't hesitate to lean on your church family and fellow believers. They're there to help you stay in the race, and you'll be surprised how much lighter the load feels when you share it.

Another vital aspect of staying in the race is remembering your "why." What motivates you to keep going? Perhaps it's the desire to serve others, to grow closer to God, or to fulfill a calling He has placed on your heart. When the road gets tough, revisiting your purpose can reignite that spark of motivation. Think of it like a runner visualizing the finish line. When you focus on your goals and the reasons behind them, you'll find renewed strength to push through. Philippians 3:14 reminds us to *"press on toward the goal."* So, keep that vision alive and let it fuel your journey!

Staying in the race is a dynamic blend of endurance, community, and purpose. As you navigate life's challenges with biblical wisdom, remember that every step you take brings you closer to God's promises. Keep your eyes on the prize, lean on your fellow runners, and don't forget to enjoy the journey. With faith as your compass and the love of Christ as your fuel, you'll find that staying in the race is not just possible—it can be a wonderfully transformative adventure!

Now, finishing the race is a concept that resonates deeply with many of us. Imagine standing at the starting line, heart racing, excitement bubbling up as you contemplate the journey ahead. The race of life isn't just about sprinting to the finish; it's about how you navigate the twists, turns, and occasional hurdles along the way. The Bible also offers a treasure trove of wisdom for those of us trying to keep our eyes on the prize while dodging distractions and setbacks.

First, let's take a moment to appreciate the joy in the journey. In Hebrews 12:1, we're encouraged to "run with perseverance the race marked out for us." This isn't just a call to endure; it's an invitation to relish every step, every mile, and yes, even every stumble. Think about it: those moments when you trip over your own feet can lead to the most memorable stories! Embracing the ups and downs means allowing ourselves to grow and learn, creating a rich tapestry of experiences that shapes who we are. So, let's not dread the obstacles; let's see them as divine detours leading us to unexpected blessings.

As we navigate the track, let's not forget about the ultimate prize at the end. Paul, in 2 Timothy 4:7-8, speaks of finishing the race and keeping the faith, assuring us that there's a crown waiting for those who persevere. While the idea of a heavenly crown might sound a tad regal, it's not about the shiny bling; it's about the recognition of a life well-lived in service and love. Picture yourself crossing that finish line, arms raised in victory, knowing you've made a difference in the lives of others. That moment is worth every ounce of effort!

Finally, let's consider the power of reflection. Just as athletes analyze their performances to improve, we too should take a moment to assess our journey. What lessons have we learned along the way? What challenges have shaped our character? Reflecting on our experiences helps us find meaning and purpose in even the most difficult moments. It's like a spiritual pit stop that allows us to refuel and reset before charging ahead. So, as we reach the final stretch, let's pause, look back, and soak in the beauty of our race, knowing that God has been with us every step of the way.

Finishing the race is less about speed and more about faithfulness. With every step we take, let's remember to enjoy the journey, lean on our fellow believers, stay focused on the ultimate prize, and reflect on our growth. As we run this beautiful race together, may we find joy in the process and strength in the Lord, ensuring that when we cross that finish line, we do so with hearts filled with gratitude and love.

Reflection Questions

- *What daily practices can you incorporate to strengthen your perseverance?*

- *How can gratitude play a role in building resilience, even during challenging times?*

- *How can keeping an eternal perspective help you endure hardships in your life right now?*

Reflection Exercise

Write a list of three daily practices you can start this week to strengthen your perseverance. These might include a daily prayer time, a gratitude journal, or reading a passage of Scripture each morning. Commit to these practices, asking God to help you grow in faith, so that you're prepared to face challenges with endurance and strength.

Conclusion: Embracing the Journey

Reflection

A S WE REACH THE end of this book, it's important to recognize that the journey of wisdom is never truly over. The questions we've explored are not just intellectual exercises—they are lived experiences that shape who we are and how we relate to God, ourselves, and others. While we may have found answers, those answers often serve as starting points for new questions, new challenges, and new revelations. And that's the beauty of wisdom—it's not a destination, but a continual pursuit.

As we come to the end of this journey, take a moment to reflect on all that you've explored. Each chapter has delved into some of life's deepest questions: *Who am I? Why do I suffer? Where is God in my pain? How can I find peace and purpose? How do I live out holiness? How do I persevere?* And others. These aren't questions with simple answers, but through each one, God has shown us that His Word holds timeless wisdom that is alive, relevant, practical, and useful for our everyday lives. Ultimately, we've sought to understand the foundational truths of our existence, navigate life's challenges with grace, and persevere on our journey of faith.

In each chapter, we've turned to the Bible, not just as a source of religious teachings, but as the ultimate guide for living a life rooted in truth, wisdom, and divine love. We've seen how Scripture speaks directly to the heart of our struggles and longings, offering us practical insights, comfort, and hope. And most importantly, we've discovered that

God is always present, always speaking, and always guiding us—even when life feels overwhelming or uncertain.

The journey of faith is often filled with questions and uncertainties, but it's also filled with hope, purpose, and peace. God has invited you into a story far greater than anything this world has to offer—a story where you are loved, valued, and called to live a life that reflects His goodness. This book has been an invitation to dig deeper, to seek God in every aspect of life, and to trust that His answers, even when they don't come all at once, are sufficient.

The journey of faith and wisdom is ongoing. As much as we may want to tie everything together neatly and have all our questions answered, life doesn't work that way. New seasons bring new challenges, and old questions sometimes resurface in unexpected ways. But through it all, we can be assured of one unchanging truth: God's wisdom is available to us at every step of the way.

The Bible reminds us that God generously gives wisdom to those who ask for it. In James 1:5, we're told, *"If any of you lacks wisdom, let him ask of God, who gives to all liberally and without reproach, and it will be given to him."* This is the invitation that stands before us as we move forward—an invitation to continue seeking, asking, and trusting that God will reveal His wisdom in every season of life.

Living Out the Wisdom You've Found

Wisdom is not passive. It's something we live out daily. The answers we've explored together are not meant to be stored away in our minds; they are meant to transform how we live, how we love, and how we serve. The Bible's wisdom is meant to be applied—to our relationships, our decisions, our trials, and our triumphs. It shapes the way we respond to the uncertainties of life and the way we reflect God's character to the world.

Living out wisdom means choosing faith over fear when the road ahead is unclear. It means choosing to love others when it's difficult and choosing to trust God when the answers don't come right away. It means embracing holiness, community, and perseverance in the face of life's challenges. This is the life God calls us to—a life that reflects His wisdom, love, and grace in every circumstance.

As we close this chapter of our journey together, I want to remind you of something essential: You are not alone. The same God who has guided you through the pages of this book is the same God who will continue to walk with you in the days, months, and years to come. He knows the questions that weigh on your heart, the fears that sometimes keep you up at night, and the dreams that you hold deep within your soul. And He cares about all of it.

God's wisdom is not a distant, impersonal force. It's an expression of His deep love for you. His wisdom is meant to guide you, comfort you, and lead you closer to His heart. And as you continue to ask questions and seek His truth, you can trust that He will be faithful to reveal Himself to you in ways that are both personal and profound.

Main Themes Revisited

Throughout this book, we've seen how God meets us right where we are, offering wisdom, comfort, and purpose in every season:

- **Identity in God:** You are created in His image, fearfully and wonderfully made. Your worth isn't based on what you do but on who you are as a child of God. In every season, you can stand firm, knowing that you are valued and cherished.

- **Purpose and Calling:** Your purpose isn't a single destination, but a daily journey of living out the Great Commission, of loving others and bringing glory to God in the unique way He's equipped you. No matter where you are, God has placed you there for a reason, and every action done in love and faithfulness has eternal significance.

- **Trust and Perseverance:** Trusting God in uncertain times isn't about having all the answers but about choosing faith over fear. Perseverance isn't just surviving hardship; it's allowing God to shape your character, deepen your faith, and prepare you for what He has in store.

- **Community and Holiness:** God hasn't called you to walk this journey alone. Community gives us strength, accountability, and support, while holiness allows us to reflect God's love and light to those around us. Together, these form a foundation that empowers us to live boldly, honoring God with our lives.

An Encouragement to Continue

This journey is just the beginning. The beauty of walking with God is that He is always ready to reveal more of Himself and guide you deeper into His truth. Every question you ask, every doubt you face, and every moment of surrender brings you closer to the One Who created you, knows you, and loves you unconditionally.

As you continue to seek Him, remember that God's Word is a wellspring of wisdom. Proverbs 2:6 reminds us, *"For the Lord gives wisdom; from His mouth come knowledge and understanding."* When life feels uncertain, when challenges arise, or when you need guidance, turn back to His Word. God's answers aren't just words on a page—they are living truths that transform, uplift, and guide.

As you move forward from this book, my prayer is that you will continue to seek God's wisdom with an open heart and a willing spirit. Don't be afraid of the questions you carry. Don't shy away from the uncertainties that arise. Instead, bring them to God, trusting that He is big enough to handle your doubts, your fears, and your hopes. He is, after all, the One Who formed you, the One Who knows the answers before you even ask the questions. Remember, the journey of faith is not about having all the answers, but about trusting the One Who does. And in that trust, you will find the peace, purpose, and wisdom you seek.

Closing Prayer

Let's close with a prayer, asking God to seal these truths in your heart as you go forward:

Heavenly Father, thank You for being the source of all wisdom and for revealing Your love, grace, and truth to us through Your Word. As we close this chapter, help us to carry the wisdom You've given into our daily lives. Teach us to trust You more deeply, to seek You in every season, and to live with purpose, peace, and joy. May Your Word be a lamp to our feet and a light to our path, guiding us each step of the way in this daily journey. In Jesus' name, Amen.

Final Reflection Exercise

As a final reflection, take a few moments to write down what God has revealed to you throughout this journey. Refer back to your notes from the previous reflection exercise and consider each of these questions:

- *What is one new truth or perspective you've gained about your identity in God?*

- *How do you feel God calling you to live out your purpose more intentionally?*

- *What areas of your life will you entrust to God, especially in times of uncertainty?*

- *How can you strengthen your community or be a light to those around you?*

This reflection is a way to anchor what you've learned and keep it close to your heart as you step into the future.

Thank You for Joining This Journey

Thank you for choosing to embark on this journey of faith and discovery. May you continue to find wisdom, purpose, and strength in God's Word, trusting that His answers are not only present, but are exactly what you need to live with confidence, courage, peace, and joy. As you move forward, remember: God's wisdom is not only found in answers, but in the journey of faith, and His presence is with you every step of the way. May you walk forward in confidence, knowing that you are found in God's love, wisdom, and grace. And may your journey of wisdom continue to lead you deeper into His truth, now and always. God bless you on your journey.

About the Author

O BED OLIVARRÍA WAS BORN in Mexicali, Mexico and spent his youth as a fully bicultural transnational citizen. He has a passion for writing both fiction and nonfiction, public speaking, composing, arranging, and performing music, as well as traveling around the world. He loves the thrill of adrenaline-pumping activities, but also the quiet reflection he gets from writing and creating.

His love for books started at an early age, as his parents were eager readers and owned thousands of books. His passion for writing was born after winning a city-wide short story competition while in high school in Arizona. The publication of this in a local journal inspired him to continue creating worlds and characters in print.

Obed has worked as a youth and young adult pastor, as a graphic designer, as a session musician, as a ministry consultant, as university dean, as school administrator, and school psychologist. Having worked at every level of the education system, from pre-k to university, has given him an expedition to the human psyche. He has a dynamic love of life and ministry, and he is a deep thinker, and an honest intellectual to the Christian gospel.

Obed lives in sunny Orange County, California with his charming wife and two energetic children. Obed hopes to continue writing inspiring books that entertain, but also challenge the status quo. Personally, he would like to visit every country in the world, drawing inspiration from these travels for another great story.

www.ingramcontent.com/pod-product-compliance
Lightning Source LLC
Chambersburg PA
CBHW071207120626
46546CB00006B/2450